Welcome to

Collection Series, 1999 Edition

Celebrating the Best-Kept Secrets from Renowned Restaurants
in the Local Area and Across the Country

Since the beginning of time, a meal has been the universal activity that transcends all languages and ethnic backgrounds. A grand meal is the canvas for celebrations of love and friendship. A fine dining experience soothes the soul, nurtures the mind, and warms the heart. Discover the wisdom of expert restaurateurs as you taste and enjoy their recipes in your own kitchen.

"Restaurant Secrets™" Collection Series, 1999 Edition

Great for cooking at home, dining out, or giving as a gift!

~ Happy Cooking and Fine Dining ~

Featured Restaurants...

Local Secrets

Famous Secrets

A La Carte

Child Friendly

Banquet Facilities

HeartSmart Menu

Credit Cards Accepted

Valet Parking

Alcohol Served

and Their Best-Kept Secrets!

Appetizers

Beef, Pork & Other Meats

Fish & Seafood

Pasta & Grains

Poultry

Soups & Salads

Vegetarian

A Message from the Restaurateurs

Come behind the closed doors of our kitchens to learn the secrets of transforming food into culinary art. Our original recipes featured in "Restaurant Secrets™" have been prepared especially for you. Each recipe includes every ingredient and preparation step, so that you can easily experience the same extraordinary results in your kitchen at home.

We hope to see you soon and look forward to hearing about your experience with these treasured recipes.

~ Wishing you many occasions of cooking and dining pleasure ~

Seattle

Voted "Best City in the West" by Money Magazine in 1998, Seattle, the largest city in the Pacific Northwest, triumphantly upholds its reputation with divine natural resources, a thriving economy and high culture. Breathtakingly set amid hills between Puget Sound and Lake Washington with a spectacular view of Mount Rainier, Seattle is the perfect spot for nature lovers. The Olympic Mountains and Cascade Ranges, offering a variety of activities like hiking, mountain climbing, skiing and water sports, surround the city in grandeur. Servicing an enormous port that is the main link with Alaska and a hub for European trade, Seattle is the region's financial, commercial and industrial hub. Home to company headquarters for powerhouses like Microsoft, the largest global personal computer software firm and Boeing, the largest aircraft manufacturer in the world, Seattle remains a strong leader in advanced technology for electronics, computer software and environmental engineering.

Host to a variety of events like Seafair, Bite of Seattle, the 1990 Goodwill Games and the Seattle International Film Festival, the city is hardly all work and no play. Musically known as the hometown to contemporary trend-setting rock and pop groups, Seattle also offers traditional sounds of the Seattle Opera and the Seattle Symphony. Woodland Park Zoo, Pike Place Market, the Seattle Center and the Space Needle, a 600-foot skyline landmark built for the World's Fair in 1962, add considerable fuel to the city's apparent liveliness.

The creativity and diversity of Seattle's population is illustrated by the variety of restaurant cuisine. Although best known for its seafood, local farm produce and its celebration of the Pacific Rim, all culinary influences are embraced. *Restaurant Secrets*™ shares signature recipes from the culinary masters in Seattle and across the country. Try these secrets in the privacy of your home and then visit the restaurants to appreciate the chefs' expertise while dining at these superior establishments.

When you purchase *Restaurant Secrets*™, many community projects can continue to operate and benefit the Seattle area since a portion of the proceeds return to local schools and non-profit organizations. Thank you for supporting your community, and please enjoy these wonderful secrets.

Bon appétit!

Garlic shrimp in Manzanilla sherry, Chile de Arbol, thyme and fresh lemon

C·A·C·T·U·S™
FOODS OF MEXICO AND THE SOUTHWEST

4220 E. Madison St., Seattle, WA
(206)324-4140

Cactus is a bustling restaurant that has pleased its guests with Mexican, Southwestern, Spanish and other Hispanic-influenced fare for years.

The 1998 Zagat Survey rated Cactus "Excellent," Seattle Times gave it "Three Stars," and Seattle Post Intelligencer rated Cactus "Three Stars." Customers and critics alike agree that Cactus is as innovative as it is affordable. You will too.

Cactus is located just minutes from Downtown Seattle.

Gambas Al Ajillo

PrepTime: 5 minutes
Cooking Time: 10 minutes
Servings Per Recipe: 4

1 Heat oil over medium-high heat in a large skillet. Add thyme and rosemary, immediately followed by the garlic and chile. Sauté until garlic is tender, but not browned. Add prawns. Simmer for 1 minute. Squeeze lemon into pan. Deglaze with sherry. Simmer for an additional minute. Serve with grilled bread and enjoy!

This dish goes well over rice or your favorite starch.

2/3 cup Spanish olive oil

4 sprigs thyme

4 sprigs rosemary

12-14 garlic cloves, chopped coarsely

8 dried Chile de Arbol

20-24 large prawns, peeled and deveined

2 lemons, quartered

1/2 cup Spanish Manzanilla sherry

Grilled bread slices (for serving)

2214 - 1st Ave., Seattle, WA (206)441-9600

When you're looking for a vibrant atmosphere, look no further than the Axis Restaurant. It's the place to see and be seen in Seattle. Owners Jim Malevitsis and Richard Malia included a street-side bar to add to the fun of people-watching.

The dual-tiered decor with its exhibition kitchen invites you to watch Chef Alvin Binuya and his team in action. Whatever you're hungry for, this restaurant can satisfy. Their eclectic menu offers everything from appetizers large enough to share with your friends, to rotisserie specials.

Rated as one of the "Top Spots" by Cuisine, Axis is a place you must try.

Tantalizing barbequed ribs...a perfect do ahead dish

Axis Five Spice Baby Back Ribs

PrepTime: 10 minutes
Cooking Time: 60 minutes
Servings Per Recipe: 4

2 quarts chicken stock

1 oz fresh ginger, coarsely chopped

1 tablespoon + 1/2 teaspoon Chinese five spice

1/2 cup + 1 tablespoon soy sauce

5 cloves garlic, crushed

5 lb baby back pork ribs

1/4 cup chili-garlic sauce

1/4 cup hoisin sauce

1/2 cup plum sauce

1 tablespoon sesame oil

Sesame seeds, toasted (to garnish)

Cilantro sprigs (to garnish)

1 **Braising Ribs:** Place chicken stock, ginger, 1 tablespoon Chinese five spice, 1/2 cup soy sauce, and garlic in a heavy pan sized so that the liquid is no less than 2 1/2-inches deep, but wide enough to accommodate the rib racks. (The rib racks can be cut in half if necessary.) Bring the liquid to a boil. Reduce heat, simmer 15 minutes. Place rib racks into simmering liquid. Braise for 30 minutes. Remove ribs from liquid, set aside to cool. Keep liquid at a simmer. Reduce by two-thirds, set aside to cool.

2 **Chinese Barbeque Sauce:** Combine chili-garlic sauce, hoisin sauce, plum sauce, 1 tablespoon soy sauce, sesame oil, and 1/2 teaspoon Chinese five spice in a nonreactive bowl. Mix well; set aside.

3 **Finishing:** Heat a grill. Place ribs on grill for 5-8 minutes or until thoroughly heated. Brush both sides of rib racks with the barbeque sauce. Continue grilling 2-3 minutes until sauce begins to brown well. Baste the ribs with barbeque sauce again. Remove from grill. Cut into the individual ribs. Place on desired serving platter, pour the hot reduced braising liquid over the ribs. Sprinkle with toasted sesame seeds and cilantro sprigs. Enjoy!

The braising and sauce portion of this recipe can be prepared up to 3 days prior. So, at the time of service, all you need to do is heat ribs over a barbeque.

Chef Amy's sweet potato and lemon grass bisque

CHEZ SHEA

SHEA'S LOUNGE

94 Pike St., Seattle, WA (206)467-9990

Leave the world behind and visit a unique hideaway in the Pike Place Market called Chez Shea. Gaze over the rooftops, watch the sun set behind the Olympics, and observe the ferries gliding across Puget Sound.

The only thing more spectacular than the view, however, is the cuisine. Chez Shea invites you to try their entrees, which are prepared with the freshest and finest foods of the Pacific Northwest. Enjoy a leisurely prix-fixe four-course dinner in the intimate, candlelit dining room. Or spend a more casual evening in Shea's Lounge which features a bistro and late-night menu; the perfect place for a before or after event repast.

Sweet Potato and Lemon Grass Bisque

PrepTime: 20 minutes
Cooking Time: 30 minutes
Servings Per Recipe: 8

1 **Thai Peanut Salsa:** Preheat oven to 375° F. Place peanuts onto a baking sheet. Roast in oven until golden. Cool. Chop with a knife or process until roughly chopped. Place into a bowl, add cilantro, sambal, and pinch of salt. Set aside.

2 **Chive Oil:** Place chives in a blender with a pinch of salt. Add olive oil and puree until smooth. Strain through a fine strainer, pushing with a spatula to press some of the solids through. Set aside.

3 **Soup:** Melt butter over low heat in a 2-quart saucepan. Add onions. Cook until soft, about 5 minutes. Avoid browning onion. Add ginger and garlic. Sauté 3 more minutes. Add sweet potatoes and just enough water to cover potatoes. Add lemon grass. Simmer until potatoes are soft. Remove from heat. Discard lemon grass. Puree soup in a food processor or blender, working in batches, if necessary. Strain through a fine mesh strainer. Add coconut milk. Mix well. Reheat soup. Add lime juice, to taste. Season with salt and pepper, to taste.

4 **Serving:** Ladle soup into warmed bowls, garnish with peanut salsa and drizzle with chive oil. Serve.

1/3 cup raw peanuts

2 tablespoons cilantro, chopped

2 tablespoons sambal oelek (available at Asian grocery store)

1 bunch chives, coarsely chopped

Pinch of salt

1/2 cup olive oil

2 tablespoons butter

1 large yellow onion, peeled and sliced

1 2-inch piece ginger, peeled and minced

2 tablespoons garlic, minced

1 1/2 lb sweet potatoes, peeled and diced

2 stalks lemon grass, split lengthwise

1 can coconut milk

Lime juice (to taste)

Salt and pepper (to taste)

A hearty vegetable stew with seasonal vegetables and turkey confit

Theoz

1523 - 6th Ave., Seattle, WA (206)749-9660

Theoz of downtown Seattle, represents the vanguard of contemporary fine dining in the Northwest. Theoz is fun and fashionable, catering to a loyal clientele who enjoy a menu that constantly adds new and intriguing dishes. The kitchen under the direction of Chet Wallenstein, creates French Country classics by using local garden-fresh produce and adding special touches.

Owners Theodora van den Beld and Gary Bocz, believe the heart of every restaurant is strengthened by its dedication to treating all customers as honored guests. As a result, they and their staff have earned a national reputation for superb food, interesting wines and warm hospitality. They invite you to join them.

Authentic Garbure

PrepTime: 60 minutes
Cooking Time: 90 minutes
Servings Per Recipe: 4

1 **Turkey Confit: (1 week process)** Rinse and dry turkey legs. Place in a large nonreactive mixing bowl. Combine salt, pepper, thyme, rosemary, ground cloves, coriander, and ginger. Rub spices over entire leg. Add 7 garlic cloves and 1 whole clove into the bowl. Cover and refrigerate overnight, 24 hours.

2 Melt fat over low heat in a large cast iron skillet. Wipe all of the salt mixture off the legs. Reserve the garlic and clove. When fat has melted, but is not hot, add turkey and reserved garlic and cloves. Cook over very low heat, approximately at 225° F for 5 hours, or until the meat is fork tender and literally falls off the bone. Remove legs from the pot. Pass fat through a fine strainer. To store the legs, use either sterilized glass jars or sterilized heavy crocks with wide tops. Arrange legs in them and pour hot fat over them, covering completely. Let cool at room temperature. Cover tightly and refrigerate at least 1 week before eating. (it can be kept up to 3 months) Remove the containers from the refrigerator a few hours before cooking, to soften the fat. Remove the turkey pieces from the fat. Reserve approximately 5 tablespoons of the rendered duck fat for Garbure.

3 **Garbure:** Heat 3 tablespoons of the rendered duck fat over medium heat in a large soup pot. Add leeks, onion, and celery. Stir well; cover; cook over low heat for 15 minutes. Do not brown vegetables. Add carrots, potatoes, and 5 cloves of garlic. (At this time, you may add seasonal vegetables, in addition to those listed.) Cook, covered, until potatoes are soft. Meanwhile, heat 2 tablespoons of the rendered duck fat over medium heat in a large pan. Add cabbage. Sauté until light brown and caramelized. Add chicken stock to soup. Cook for 30-40 minutes. Taste and adjust seasonings with salt and pepper. Ten minutes before serving, add turkey leg confit and Italian parsley. Simmer 10 minutes. To serve, ladle meat and vegetables into soup plates, then pour soup broth over. Enjoy!

4 turkey legs, about 1 lb each
2 tablespoons kosher salt
1 teaspoon black pepper
2 teaspoons thyme
2 teaspoons rosemary
2 teaspoons ground cloves
2 teaspoons ground coriander
2 teaspoons ground ginger
12 whole garlic cloves, peeled
1 whole clove
1 quart duck fat
2 leeks, white parts only, chopped
1 medium onion, sliced
2 celery stalks, chopped
2 carrots, sliced
3 Yukon gold potatoes, quartered
1/2 head savoy cabbage, sliced
1 1/2 quarts chicken stock
1/2 cup Italian flat parsley, chopped
Salt and pepper (to taste)
Seasonal vegetables (as desired)

With soft cooked quail eggs and chive oil

THE PAINTED TABLE

92 Madison St., Seattle, WA (206)624-3646

"Food as art" is a familiar concept, but a restaurant design that focuses on art to complement the food is something else entirely. That's the idea at The Painted Table Restaurant — to provide a unique visual setting that whets the appetite for what's to come. Its contemporary atmosphere provides a fitting backdrop for the work of local Northwest artists.

In the kitchen, Chef Tim Kelley creates art of another kind, bringing over thirteen years of experience to The Painted Table. The cuisine is faithful to the Pacific Northwest, combining traditional French cooking with contemporary Asian and American touches. Seasonal menus feature unique combinations of local herbs, vegetables, seafood and regional favorites. House specialties are the Layered Goat Cheese and Vegetable Salad with Grilled Eggplant, and the Honey-Lavendar Duck. These entrees, plus others, have earned an excellent Three Star rating from the Seattle Post-Intelligencer.

Sliced Artichoke and Dungeness Crab Salad

PrepTime: 30 minutes
Cooking Time: 30 minutes
Servings Per Recipe: 4

1 **Poaching Artichokes:** Clean artichokes and cover with water and lemon juice. In a medium pot, heat 2 tablespoons olive oil over medium heat. Add onions, carrots, and celery; cook until tender. In another medium pot, add garlic, tomato paste, and flour. Mix well. Add artichokes and lemon water. Season with salt and pepper, to taste. Add rosemary, thyme, oregano, and bay leaf. Cook until tender. Remove and bring to room temperature. Reserve liquid. Clean artichoke hearts. Slice 4 of the hearts twice horizontally, making 3 pieces from each heart. Puree the remaining artichoke heart with 2 tablespoons of the poaching liquid. Set aside.

2 **Artichoke Sauce:** Place the artichoke puree and mustard in a bowl. Whisk in 5 tablespoons of olive oil, forming an emulsion. Add vinegar and season with salt and pepper to taste. Set aside.

3 **Chive Oil:** Puree 2 tablespoons chives and 3 tablespoons olive oil in a blender for 10 seconds. Set aside.

4 **Crab:** Toss crab with basil, 1/2 teaspoon chives, and shallots. Add 2 tablespoons artichoke sauce and 1 tablespoon olive oil. Season with salt and pepper to taste.

5 **Assemble:** Spoon a little sauce into the center of the plate. Place a slice of artichoke down and spoon a little crab on top. Continue process with remaining 2 slices of artichoke, ending with crab on top. Perch quail egg on top. Garnish with basil. Drizzle artichoke sauce around the plate, followed by chive oil. Repeat with remaining 3 plates.

5 medium artichokes

Water (as needed)

Juice of 2 lemons

9 tablespoons olive oil (divided)

1 onion, sliced

1 carrot, sliced

2 stalks celery, sliced

3 cloves garlic, smashed

1 tablespoon tomato paste

2 tablespoons flour

Salt and pepper (to taste)

2 sprigs rosemary

2 sprigs thyme

2 sprigs oregano

1 bay leaf

1 teaspoon Dijon mustard

2 tablespoons red wine vinegar

2 1/2 tablespoons chives, chopped

12 oz fresh Dungeness crab, cooked

1 teaspoon basil, chopped

1/2 tablespoon shallots, chopped

4 quail eggs (boil for 2 minutes), peeled and halved

Basil leaves (to garnish)

A variation of tomatoes perfect for the start of any meal

1101 - 4th Ave., Seattle, WA
(206)624-7755

Reportedly named after America's first cocktail, the Sazerac Restaurant continues to be an establishment of firsts. Warm jewel-like colors, cozy mahogany booths and velvet curtains contrast with the more contemporary elements of stained concrete floors and whimsical artwork. The lively atmosphere is accentuated by an elevated kitchen and its wood-burning oven, rotisserie and grill.

American Cuisine with Southern inspirations are the natural tendencies of Louisiana-born Chef Jan Birnbaum. So, at Sazerac, you'll find Fried Catfish with Mardi Gras Slaw; Pork Porterhouse with Soft and Sexy Grits, Pickled Cabbage and New Orleans Gravy; and Spit-Roasted Whole Fish with Lemon Chili Broth, Escarole and Orzo highlighting the menu. Chef Birnbaum and Executive Chef Bryan Weener work in concert to create tempting dishes that will amaze your palate.

Sazerac has been hailed by local and national publications. Visit them soon.

Tomatoes in all of their Glory

PrepTime: 60 minutes
Cooking Time: 60 minutes
Servings Per Recipe: 6

3/4 cup extra virgin olive oil (divided)

1 cup balsamic vinegar

Salt and pepper (to taste)

1 large red onion, peeled

1 shallot, minced

1 clove garlic, minced

3 tablespoons fresh lemon juice

2 1/4 teaspoons kosher salt

1/8 teaspoon cracked black pepper

1 cup all-purpose flour

1 cup cornmeal

1/2 teaspoon cayenne pepper

oil (for frying)

2 hard green unripe tomatoes, cut 1/2-inch thick

1 cup buttermilk

6 assorted beautiful large vine ripe tomatoes, cut 1/2-inch thick

20 small sweet 100's, or pear tomatoes, cut in half

6 Bocconcini (small balls of mozzarella)

Small amount of favorite greens*

*Chef prefers frisée and fresh basil leaves

1 Keep tomatoes at room temperature for a full day. About 1 hour before serving, wash and place in refrigerator. This will give them a pleasant coolness while allowing them to have their greatest flavor.

2 **Red Onions:** Combine 1/4 cup olive oil, 1/4 cup balsamic vinegar and salt and pepper in a nonreactive bowl. Mix well. Cut red onion into 1/2-inch thick round slices. Keep slices intact. Gently toss in the marinade. Leave at room temperature for an hour or refrigerate overnight. Toss occasionally to evenly marinate. Heat a grill. Grill thick onion slices over high heat (a small amount of smoke and flame are desired). Turn onions over and continue grilling for about 1 minute. Leave onions crunchy and with a good purple color. Cool on flat pan in refrigerator. Store in marinade.

3 **Balsamic Reduction:** Reduce 1/2 cup balsamic vinegar over medium heat in a small nonreactive saucepan to a light syrup stage. Reserve in a small dish (ceramic ramekin).

4 **Vinaigrette:** Combine shallots, garlic, lemon juice, 1/4 cup balsamic vinegar, 1/4 teaspoon kosher salt, and 1/8 teaspoon cracked black pepper in a nonreactive bowl. Mix well. Whisk in 1/2 cup olive oil. Reserve at room temperature.

5 **Fried Green Tomatoes:** Heat a deep fryer to 350° F. Mix flour, cornmeal, cayenne, and 2 teaspoons kosher salt in a nonreactive bowl. Place sliced green tomatoes in buttermilk, then dredge in flour/cornmeal mixture. Fry tomatoes until they float and are crispy on the outside, or beginning to slightly soften on the inside if pan frying. Remove to paper towel or lined drain pan to remove excess oil. Reserve in a warm place.

6 **Finishing:** Combine remaining tomatoes in a large nonreactive bowl. Separate red onions into rings; add to bowl. Add cheese and the vinaigrette. Sprinkle with salt and pepper. Gently toss.

7 On six cold plates arrange tomatoes, fried green tomatoes, red onions, and cheese. Dress a small amount of your favorite greens in the oil and tomato juices left in the mixing bowl. Place small sprigs of the greens on top each salad. With a small spoon (demitase) drizzle some of the balsamic reduction around the tomatoes on the plate. Enjoy!

With baby vegetables and chanterelle mushrooms

Hunt Club

900 Madison St., Seattle, WA (206)343-6156

In Seattle's restaurant scene where cigar bars and steak restaurants are the order of the day, the Hunt Club is a beloved institution with a fresh approach. Adherence to the philosophy of simple ingredients and comforting favorites is what makes the Hunt Club so special. Diners are invited to linger over their meal in a friendly and lush environment whether it's for breakfast, lunch or dinner.

Chef Brian Scheehser has been instrumental in the restaurant's newly emerged menu direction. "Hunt Club Cuisine is best described as 'Northwest Mediterranean Cuisine'," explains Chef Scheehser. "Incomparable ingredients, like the freshest vegetables and simple, flavorful herbs create classically Northwest dishes with an unabashed borrowing of Mediterranean kitchen staples such as fresh paprika and thyme, roasted Roma tomatoes and kalamata olives." To complement the new menu, the restaurant's wine cellar has been completely restocked with a selection of enticing wines from top international vineyards.

Osso Bucco

PrepTime: 30 minutes
Cooking Time: 120 minutes
Servings Per Recipe: 6

- 1/2 cup olive oil
- 6 osso bucco, cut 2 1/2-inches
- Salt and pepper (to taste)
- 1 yellow onion, roughly chopped
- 2 carrots, roughly chopped
- 2 stalks celery, roughly chopped
- 4 thyme sprigs
- 2 bay leaves
- 2 tablespoons tomato paste
- 1 cup red wine
- 4 cups veal stock
- 12 baby carrots, peeled
- 12 pearl onions, peeled
- 12 green beans
- 12 asparagus spears
- 1 cup chanterelle mushrooms, sliced
- 2 tomatoes, peeled, seeded and roughly chopped

1 **Osso bucco:** Preheat oven to 350° F. Heat olive oil over medium-high heat in a heavy frying pan. Add osso bucco. Sear until golden brown. Turn and season with salt and pepper. Remove to large casserole, arranging osso bucco in a single layer.

2 **Sauce:** Place the roughly cut onion, carrot, celery, thyme, and bay leaves into a frying pan. Sauté briefly over medium heat. Add tomato paste and cook briefly. Add red wine. Reduce by half. Add veal stock and heat to a simmer. Season with salt and pepper, to taste. Pour mixture over the osso bucco and cover. Cook in oven for approximately 2 hours, or until osso bucco is fully cooked. When ready, remove osso bucco from pan. Strain liquid into a saucepan. Reduce slightly; adjust seasonings with salt and pepper, to taste.

3 **Vegetables:** Blanch carrots, onions, green beans, and asparagus. Sauté mushrooms and tomatoes over medium-high heat in a large sauté pan. Season with salt and pepper, to taste.

4 **Serving:** Place osso bucco in a large bowl. Cover with a little sauce and garnish with vegetables, mushrooms and tomatoes. Serve.

Quail over a bed of arugula with carrot essence and port wine

SALISH
LODGE & SPA

6501 Railroad Ave. S.E., Snoqualmie, WA
(425)888-2556

Located thirty miles east of Seattle, Salish Lodge & Spa enjoys a breathtaking view of the majestic 268-foot Snoqualmie Falls. Northwest Cuisine is a natural choice in this setting, emphasizing seasonal availability and freshness. Noted for his exceptional "culinary simplicity" Executive Chef William Belickis allows the essence of the primary ingredients to speak for themselves. He prepares an ever-changing menu to capture these quality ingredients at the height of their seasons. With a wine list that features over 500 labels, the Salish Lodge Restaurant creates an experience unequalled in the area.

The restaurant received AAA's Four Diamond Award as well as a Four Star rating from the Mobil Travel Guide. It has also been a five-year recipient of the DiRoNA Award for Distinguished Country Breakfast.

Please drop by the Salish Lodge & Spa. The experience will be well worth the trip.

Seared Oregon Quail

PrepTime: 25 minutes
Cooking Time: 15 minutes
Servings Per Recipe: 2

1 Rub the quail with nutmeg, clove, orange zest, and 1 teaspoon olive oil. Set aside for 15 minutes.

2 **Carrot essence:** Heat carrot juice over medium-high heat in a non-reactive saucepan. Bring to a simmer. Add ginger. Simmer until the juice becomes syrupy. Place into a blender with the butter. Blend until smooth. Set aside; keep warm.

3 **Port wine reduction:** Heat port wine over medium-high heat in a small non-reactive saucepan. Bring to a simmer. Reduce until wine has a syrupy consistency. Set aside.

4 **Quail:** Heat 1 tablespoon olive oil over medium-high heat. Season quail with salt and pepper. Add to pan. Brown both sides of the quail, and cook until the legs are juicy, but no longer red inside. Keep warm.

5 **Arugula:** Heat 2 tablespoons of olive oil over medium-high heat. Add shallots and arugula. Sauté until tender. Season with salt and pepper, to taste.

6 **Serving:** Place arugula on serving plates. Top with quail. Spoon the carrot essence around the arugula. Garnish with drizzles of port wine reduction. Enjoy.

2 quails, semi boneless

1 pinch nutmeg

1 clove

1/2 teaspoon orange zest

3 tablespoons + 1 teaspoon olive oil

2 cups carrot juice

1 small piece ginger

2 oz butter

1 cup port wine

Salt and pepper (to taste)

1 bunch arugula

1 shallot, chopped

A tantalizing crab appetizer

Ray's boathouse

6049 Seaview Ave. N.W., Seattle, WA
(206)789-3770

A panoramic view of Puget Sound and the Olympic Mountains is just one of the feasts that Ray's Boathouse presents to its guests. The other treat is the innovative menu that Chef Charles Ramseyer provides.

Whether you dine in the downstairs Boathouse Dining Room or in the more casual upstairs Cafe, your eyes and your tastebuds will be richly rewarded. Selected wines from the Northwest are available to complement your meal.

National publications recognize Ray's Boathouse as one of the best. The Zagat Survey gave it an excellent rating. Comments such as, "one of the 10 best seafood restaurants in the country" and "visiting Seattle without dining at Ray's would be like visiting Paris and missing the Eiffel Tower," are echoed year after year. All of which explains why Ray's is a favorite spot for special events, meetings and romantic dinners. Dinner reservations recommended.

Black Pepper Dungeness Crab

PrepTime: 15 minutes
Cooking Time: 30 minutes
Servings Per Recipe: 2

2 tablespoons ground black pepper

2 lb whole live Dungeness crab

4 tablespoons peanut oil

4 cloves garlic, crushed

4 tablespoons Chinese cooking rice wine (or sherry)

2 tablespoons soy sauce

1/2 tablespoon sugar

4 tablespoons fish stock or chicken stock

1 tablespoon cornstarch or cornflour

5 green onions, cut into 2-inch sticks

1 Wrap ground black pepper in cheese cloth. Boil pepper in water for 10 minutes. Cool and discard water. Set pepper aside.

2 Remove large shell of crab and discard fibrous tissue found under the shell. Divide each crab into 4 portions. Break each body in half and separate large claws from body. Leave legs attached to body.

3 Heat oil in wok or large frying pan over high heat. Add crab and fry pieces until red colored, about 10 minutes. Add crushed garlic. Roast until golden. Add rice wine, soy sauce, sugar, boiled black pepper, fish stock and bring to a simmer. Mix cornstarch with enough cold water to make a paste and add to simmering stock. Add green onions and serve with steamed Thai rice on hot platter. Garnish with green onions.

You can use cooked crab, sautéing in a wok for 5-7 minutes before adding garlic.

Served with Moroccan couscous and natural sauce

ADRIATICA

CUCINA MEDITERRANEA

1107 Dexter Ave. N., Seattle, WA
(206)285-5000

Adriatica began with Owners Connie and James Malevitsis' desire to create a restaurant resembling a rustic and romantic Mediterranean villa. A magazine article noted, "this charming converted 1930's bungalow continues to captivate with its unparalleled ambience and Mediterranean-inspired cuisine."

Blending the freshest ingredients the Northwest has to offer with an elegant dining atmosphere is what the Adriatica Restaurant offers you. Their menu showcases a variety of seafood, pasta, meat and poultry prepared with a Mediterranean influence. To complement this wonderful and diverse menu, Seattle's top wine steward, Robert McFadden designed an extensive wine list which includes over 150 wines.

Since opening in 1980, Adriatica has been named "Best Mediterranean Cuisine" by the Zagat Survey 1997, "All Time Favorite" by Seattle Magazine 1995, and "Reader's Favorite" by Gourmet Magazine 1996 and 1998.

Braised Lamb Shanks

PrepTime: 180 minutes
Cooking Time: 150 minutes
Servings Per Recipe: 6-8

6-8 lamb shanks

2 cups flour

Salt and pepper (as needed)

1/4 cup olive oil

2 onions, peeled and diced

4 carrots, peeled and diced

4 celery stalks, diced

5 garlic cloves, peeled

4 tablespoons tomato paste

1 gallon veal stock

10 parsley stems

10 thyme sprigs

1 teaspoon saffron

1 gallon water

6 cups Israeli couscous

1/2 cup apples, peeled, cored and finely diced

1/2 cup red pepper, cored, seeded and finely diced

1/4 cup almonds, chopped

1 bunch cilantro, chopped

1 bunch mint, chopped

1 tablespoon chili powder

1 tablespoon cumin

1 tablespoon butter

1 large rosemary sprig (to garnish)

1 **Shanks:** Preheat oven to 450° F. Dredge shanks in flour seasoned liberally with salt and pepper. Heat 1/4 cup oil over medium-high heat in a cast iron skillet. When hot, add shanks. Brown until golden. Place onions, carrots, celery, garlic, and tomato paste in a large sauté pan. Caramelize over medium heat. Combine shanks, vegetables, stock, parsley stems, and thyme in a 4-inch roasting pan. Cover. Bake for 2 to 2 1/2 hours or until meat is very tender. When finished, pull out shanks and strain sauce. Reserve 2 cups sauce for couscous. Reduce remaining sauce slightly.

2 **Couscous:** Bring saffron and 1 gallon water to a boil. Add couscous. Cook until al dente. Drain well. Combine couscous, apple, red pepper, almonds, cilantro, mint, chili powder, and cumin in a large, heat-proof bowl. Season with salt and pepper, to taste. Add 2 cups reserved sauce. Heat on stove. Finish couscous with 1 tablespoon (pat) of butter.

3 **Serving:** Spoon couscous in center of each bowl. Place hot shank on top. Pour reduced sauce over the shank and couscous. Garnish with large rosemary sprig.

Crabmeat tossed in penne with a creamy curry sauce

3014 - 3rd Ave. N., Seattle, WA
(206)284-3000

The Ponti Seafood Grill has been rated as one of the "Top Seafood Restaurants" in the Seattle area. Maybe it's because each entree is imaginatively prepared in a "fusion" style of cooking. Maybe it's their sophisticated and contemporary setting. Whatever the reason, Ponti is an excellent choice when you're in the mood for seafood.

Relax in the fireplace lounge or dine on the outdoor patio. Either place offers you a great view of the seaway traffic, passing along the Ship Canal.

Sunday Brunches are always fun at Ponti, so plan to join them soon.

Ponti Thai Curry Penne

PrepTime: 20 minutes
Cooking Time: 25 minutes
Servings Per Recipe: 2

1/2 cup rice vinegar

1 teaspoon ginger, grated

1/4 cup brown sugar

2 teaspoons lemon juice

1 can (16 oz) pear tomatoes, drained and chopped

1 clove

1 stick cinnamon

Salt and pepper (to taste)

1 tablespoon butter

1 teaspoon garlic, chopped

1/4 cup onion, diced

1 large Granny Smith apple, cored and diced

2 teaspoons curry powder

1/4 teaspoon salt

1 cup Marsala wine

1 cup chicken broth

3 teaspoons red-Thai curry paste

2 teaspoons Thai fish sauce

1 cup coconut milk

1 cup whipping cream

1/2 lb penne pasta (cooked according to package directions)

1/4 lb crabmeat

Fresh basil, chopped (to garnish)

1 **Chutney:** Combine vinegar, ginger, brown sugar, and lemon juice in a 1-quart saucepan. Bring to a simmer over medium heat. Simmer 5 minutes. Add tomatoes, clove, and cinnamon stick. Season with salt and pepper, to taste. Simmer 30 minutes more. Remove from heat and set aside.

2 **Curry:** Combine butter, garlic, onion, apple, curry, salt and pepper, to taste in a large saucepan. Sauté over high heat until onions are soft. Add Marsala wine. Mix well; reduce by half. Add the chicken broth, red-Thai curry paste and fish sauce. Mix well; simmer 10 minutes. Let cool. Puree in a blender or food processor. Transfer back to the saucepan. Add the coconut milk and cream. Cook over medium heat until thickened, about 10-15 minutes.

3 **Finishing:** Add pasta and crabmeat to sauce. Divide between 2 plates and top with the tomato chutney and fresh basil. Enjoy!

There is enough sauce for three-fourths to one pound of pasta.

Sturgeon served with a walnut sauce and a pepper herb relish

MARCO'S Supperclub

2510 - 1st Ave., Seattle, WA (206)441-7801

Marco's Supperclub is located in the heart of Belltown, an eclectic neighborhood which directly reflects the nature of the food, staff, atmosphere and clientele. Owners Donna Moodie and Marco Rulff created a cozy place where guests could enjoy a thoughtfully prepared meal that was also fun.

The cuisine gleans its inspiration from both the traditional and the adventuresome. Executive Chef Matthew Burian builds each dish from the flavorful goodness of great ingredients and harmonious herbs. Steak Frites, Asian Ahi Tuna, Russian-inspired Grilled Sturgeon and Flash Fried Sage Leaves all find a home on the menu.

Late diners find Marco's a pleasant place to go whether they are stopping in after the theatre, or just stopping in. A "secret" back patio, bordered by homey flowers and vines is a great retreat on summer evenings.

Sturgeon Satsivi

PrepTime: 60 minutes
Cooking Time: 10 minutes
Servings Per Recipe: 6-8

- 3/4 cup walnuts
- 3 tablespoon olive oil
- 1/2 cup onion, diced
- 6 cloves garlic
- 1/2 cinnamon stick
- 1 bay leaf
- 2 teaspoons coriander, toasted and pressed through a fine mesh strainer to remove husk
- 1 clove
- 2 teaspoons Hungarian hot paprika
- 1 bunch cilantro
- 1 tablespoon white wine vinegar
- 2 tablespoons pomegranate concentrate or pomegranate molasses (found in Indian food shops or can substitute molasses)
- 2-3 cups hot tap water
- Salt (to taste)
- 1-2 serrano chiles, chopped, seed in
- 1 large red bell pepper, cored, seeded and chopped
- 1 bunch parsley, excess stems cut off
- 1/2 bunch mint, leaves only
- 4 1/2 lb Yukon Gold potatoes, peeled and quartered
- 1 1/4 to 1 1/2 cups heavy cream
- 4 oz unsalted butter
- Pepper (to taste)
- 2 teaspoons fenugreek, toasted and ground
- 2 teaspoons caraway, toasted and ground
- 6-8 (6 ounce) sturgeon filets

1 **Walnut Sauce:** Toast walnuts in 400° F oven for 5-7 minutes. While nuts are toasting, sauté onions with 4 cloves garlic, cinnamon, and bay leaf with 1 tablespoon olive oil, over medium-high heat in a medium sauté pan. When onions become translucent, add coriander, clove, and paprika, then stir. Add walnuts and turn off heat. Mix well. Pour into processor. Run until fairly smooth. Add cilantro with motor running. Add vinegar, 1 tablespoon pomegranate concentrate and water. Return to stove and simmer on low. Add salt to taste, about 2 teaspoons.

2 **Pepper and Herb Relish:** Process chiles, pepper, and 2 cloves garlic in processor. With motor running, add herbs and 1 tablespoon pomegranate concentrate. Chill.

3 **Yukon Gold Mashed Potatoes:** Place the potatoes in a large pot with cold water to cover by 1 inch. Bring to a boil. When tender, drain well. Mash potatoes with heavy cream and butter. Season with salt and pepper to taste.

4 **Sturgeon:** Thoroughly combine toasted fenugreek and caraway. Season sturgeon filets with mix. Heat a sauté pan over medium heat. Add 2 tablespoons olive oil. When oil is hot, add filets. Pan sear 3-4 minutes on each side or until done.

5 **Serving:** Place mashed potatoes in the center of each plate. Ladle sauce around the mashed potatoes. Spoon 3 individual spoonfuls of relish equally around the mashed potatoes. Top with a filet. Serve with your favorite vegetable. Enjoy!

2010 - 4th Ave., Seattle, WA (206)441-1399

Mauro Golmarvi's love for all things Italian shines through at Assaggio.

Its ambience is the first sign of Golmarvi's passion. This popular downtown Seattle restaurant is reminiscent of a classic Italian church with high ceilings, Michelangelo-inspired frescos and elegant archways.

Your palate will quickly discern the second sign. An extensive menu of central Italian fare and Italian wine rewards you with the blends of textures and full-bodied flavors that you will want to savor forever.

Over the years, Assaggio has received top honors such as, Seattle Magazine's Readers' Choice Award 1998 Finalist "Best Italian Restaurant," Seattle Weekly's Readers' Poll 1997 "Best Italian Restaurant" and ranked on Zagat's 1996, 1997 and 1998 "Top Seattle Restaurants" list. They also received the Award of Excellence from Wine Spectator Magazine.

Free range veal chop stuffed with prosciutto, sage, and fontina

Costolette di Vitello al Portobello

PrepTime: 35 minutes
Cooking Time: 45 minutes
Servings Per Recipe: 8

6-7 tablespoons butter, unsalted

1 cup onions, diced

2 cups Italian Arborio rice

1 3/4 cups Barolo wine

2 cups water

3 cups veal stock

Salt and pepper (as needed)

1/4 cup olive oil

4 cloves garlic, coarsley chopped

4 medium Portobello mushrooms, stemmed and sliced 1/4-inch

Flour (as needed)

8 veal rib chops, trimmed, frenched 2-inches from eye

4 slices prosciutto, thinly sliced

4 slices fontina, thinly sliced

16 sage leaves, whole

1 **Risotto:** Melt 3 tablespoons butter over medium-high heat in a 12-inch, heavy bottomed sauté pan. Add onions. Sauté until translucent. Add rice. Continue to sauté, stirring constantly for 3-4 minutes. Add 1 cup wine and 1 cup water. Continuing to stir constantly until all of the water has been absorbed. Stir in 1 cup veal stock and 1 tablespoon butter. Season with salt and pepper, to taste. Simmer until rice is just cooked and has a creamy texture. Set aside.

2 **Sauce:** Heat 1/4 cup olive oil over medium-high heat in a 12-inch heavy bottomed sauté pan. Add garlic and salt and pepper, to taste. Sauté garlic until golden brown. Add Portobello mushrooms. Sauté for a minute, then add 3/4 cup wine. Reduce wine by half. Add 2 cups veal stock. Reduce by two-thirds. Stir in 2-3 tablespoons butter, rolled in flour. Continue to cook until sauce is fairly thick and shiny. Set aside; keep warm.

3 **Veal Chop:** Lay the veal chop flat on a cutting board with the bone facing up and the meat to the right. Make an opening in the side of the chop to the bone. Carefully hollow out the inside to about 1/4-inch from the edges. Do not pierce the sides. Repeat for the seven remaining chops. Stack the prosciutto, fontina and sage leaves and fold over once. Stuff each of the chops making sure that the stuffing is spread evenly through it. Brush with olive oil and season with salt and pepper. Grill until medium to medium-well, about 4-6 minutes per side. This time will vary according to the size of the veal chop.

4 **Serving:** It is best to have the sauce and risotto almost ready when starting to grill the chops. When the chops are finished. Place one-eighth of the risotto in the center of each plate. Put a veal chop on each mound of risotto with the bone side facing in. Divide the sauce equally among the eight plates. (If the sauce has become too dry, add water or more veal stock.)

Salty's famous blackened salmon and Caesar salad

1936 Harbor Ave. S.W., Seattle, WA
(206)937-1600

28201 Redondo Beach Dr. S., Redondo, WA
(253)946-0636

3839 N.E. Marine Dr., Portland, OR
(503)288-4444

Just eight minutes from downtown, is a restaurant that stands in a class by itself: that's Salty's on Alki Beach. Salty's offers world-class seafood, USDA prime steaks, plus other gourmet specialties with a spectacular view. In fact, Seattle Post Intelligencer Critic, John Owen wrote, "The view is not only the best in Seattle, this is one of the world's great view restaurants...." Of the food he said, "...the best salmon preparation I've encountered...." A sunshine deck allows you to take it all in.

Salty's other Washington location in Redondo Beach offers a striking view of Puget Sound and the Olympic Mountains. The best seafood, burgers and the friendliest service on the beach can be found there. Deck dining is available so that the entire panoramic view can be appreciated while you dine.

Salty's also has a location on the Columbia River in Portland, Oregon. Great food- great view- great service: you can find it all at Salty's.

Blackened Salmon

PrepTime: 20 minutes
Cooking Time: 15 minutes
Servings Per Recipe: 4

1 **Dressing:** Place garlic, lemon juice, red wine vinegar, 1/2 tablespoon grated Parmesan cheese, Tabasco, Worcestershire, sugar, small pinch of salt and pepper, dry mustard, and anchovies into a food processor or blender. Puree on medium speed until smooth and spices are dissolved. Slowly add mayonnaise, to prevent lumping. Continue mixing until dressing is smooth. Can be kept refrigerated for 2 days. This makes 1 cup.

2 **Salmon:** Preheat oven to 500° F. Use a nonstick spray to coat a shallow baking dish. Set aside. Pour blackening spice into a shallow plate. Dredge fish in blackening spice. Heat a heavy frying pan over high heat until a drop of water dances on the surface. Brush surface lightly with olive oil. Place salmon in hot pan. Cook approximately 2 minutes on one side (the surface of the filet will be reddish brown - not black - in appearance). Turn carefully and cook for 2 more minutes. Promptly remove filets and place in the baking dish. Bake 8-10 minutes per inch of thickness, measured at the thickest part. When done, fish should be moist and flake easily with a fork.

3 **Finishing Caesar Salad:** Combine lettuce with dressing, toss well. Divide equally among four salad bowls. Sprinkle with Parmesan and croutons. Slice each salmon and place atop each salad. Garnish with twisted lemon slices.

1 1/2 tablespoons garlic, chopped

2 tablespoons lemon juice

1/4 cup red wine vinegar

1/2 tablespoon Parmesan cheese, grated

Dash of Tabasco sauce

1/2 tablespoon Worcestershire sauce

3/4 teaspoon sugar

Small pinch of salt

Small pinch of black pepper

1/2 tablespoon dry mustard

1/2 tablespoon anchovies, finely chopped

1/2 cup mayonnaise

Olive oil (as needed)

4 oz blackening spices (Salty's blackening spices at restaurants)

4 8-ounce salmon filets

1 lb romaine lettuce, washed and rough cut

1/2 cup croutons

2 oz Parmesan cheese, shredded

4 lemon slices

With caramelized garlic and sage served over lemon risotto

1100 - 5th Ave., Seattle, WA
(206)624-5500

Part Tuscan countryside restaurant and part urban trattoria, the Tulio surrounds diners in a setting that exudes warmth with its terra cotta peach tones. Familiar comforts create a cozy ambience, while the exhibition kitchen and its wood-burning oven invite onlookers to the culinary activities.

Tulio's definition of Italian Cuisine is simple and rustic, using only the freshest local ingredients. Executive Chef Walter Pisano learned his craft in Europe and studied under Chef Jean-Louis Palladin in Washington, D.C. Baccala, Potato and Roasted Garlic Cake with Onion Preserves and Homemade Crispy Flatbread, Black Peppered Pork Loin with Fennel Gratin and Vin Santo Sauce, Roasted Mushroom filled Pansotti with Prosciutto, Pecorino Romano and double Mushroom Brodo, and Smoked Salmon-Filled Ravioli with Asparagus and Lemon Cream Sauce are some of the house specialties.

Tulio has been receiving rave reviews from customers and critics alike since it opened its doors in 1992. Bon Appétit highly recommends visiting them.

Roasted Chicken

PrepTime: 15 minutes
Cooking Time: 30 minutes
Servings Per Recipe: 4

1 **Caramelize Garlic:** Blanch garlic in boiling water for 1 minute. Heat sugar over medium heat in a small heavy sauce pan until golden brown. Remove from heat. Add blanched garlic and 2 tablespoons butter. Mix well. Set aside to cool.

2 **Chicken:** Preheat oven to 375° F. Carefully pull up the skin in one corner, at the thickest point. Slip approximately 1/2 teaspoon caramelized garlic and sage under the skin, being certain to keep skin attached on the sides as much as possible. Season chicken with salt and pepper, to taste. Heat olive oil over medium-high heat in a large sauté pan. Add chicken, skin side down. Sear until golden brown. Turn over and place in oven. Roast for approximately 15-20 minutes. When done allow chicken to rest 4-5 minutes before slicing.

3 **Lemon Risotto:** Heat 2 tsp. butter over medium heat in a large saucepan. Add shallots. Sauté until tender. Add bay leaf and rice. Coat rice with the butter and slowly add three quarters of warm chicken stock. Stir semi-continuously, adding stock as needed until rice is tender and "creamy, not soupy". Add lemon juice, preserves, zest, and Italian parsley. Season with salt and pepper, to taste.

4 **Serving:** Place risotto evenly among 4 plates. Slice each chicken and place over risotto. Enjoy!

16 cloves garlic, peeled and sliced paper thin

1 cup sugar

2 1/2 tablespoons unsalted butter

4 chicken breast, skin on (wing bone in or boneless)

9-10 fresh sage leaves, chopped

Salt and pepper (to taste)

1/4 cup olive oil

1 teaspoon shallots, minced

1 bay leaf

10 oz arborio rice

3 1/2 cups chicken stock, warm

1/2 teaspoon fresh lemon juice

1 teaspoon preserved lemon

1 teaspoon lemon zest

2 teaspoons fresh Italian parsley

219 - 4th Ave. N., Seattle, WA (206)443-2100

A local tradition and a visitor's delight, the Seattle Space Needle Restaurant is the best place in town to take in the view and savor a delicious meal. Located on the revolving 500-foot level of Seattle's most famous landmark, the Space Needle delivers a one-of-a-kind dining experience.

Panoramic views of Puget Sound, the Olympic and Cascade Mountain Ranges, Mt. Rainier, and downtown Seattle surround guests as they sample fresh, distinctive Northwest Cuisine. The seasonal menus reflect the best flavors of the Northwest, offering the freshest seafood, local vegetables and fine-aged meats. Children and adults alike, will marvel at the dessert tray which features the World Famous Lunar Orbiter Dessert; a mouthwatering ice-cream creation theatrically served over a bed of dry ice.

Open 365 days a year, the Space Needle also offers Sunday Brunch. Groups and special events welcomed.

Breaded halibut over stone ground mustard creme sauce

Emerald City Halibut

PrepTime: 15 minutes
Cooking Time: 10 minutes
Servings Per Recipe: 2

1/4 teaspoon butter

1/4 teaspoon shallots, minced

1/2 cup Chablis

1 1/4 cup heavy cream

1 tablespoon stone ground mustard

Salt and pepper (to taste)

1 egg

1/2 cup flour

1/2 cup panko breadcrumbs (Japanese bread crumbs)

2 (6-ounce) Alaskan halibut filets

1/4 cup canola oil

1 **Sauce:** Melt butter over medium-low heat in a small saucepan. Sweat the minced shallot for a minute and deglaze with Chablis wine. Reduce the wine for one minute then add the 1 cup cream, reduce by half. Finish with the stone ground mustard and salt and pepper, to taste. Set aside; keep warm.

2 **Halibut:** Beat egg and 1/4 cup cream together in a bowl. Blend flour, breadcrumbs, and salt and pepper, to taste together and place on a plate. Dip the halibut filets in the egg wash mixture then pat in the breadcrumb mixture until completely coated. Preheat a sauté pan over medium heat, add the oil to the pan, then the halibut filets and sauté about 3 minutes each side or until golden brown on the outside. Ladle sauce on plate then lay fish on top. Serve with your favorite accompaniments. The restaurant suggests roasted garlic mashed potatoes, asparagus au beurre with roasted red pepper strips.

Salmon in Japanese vegetables and tofu with Emerald Sauce

1900 - 5th Ave., Seattle, WA (206)322-4641

The Nikko Restaurant offers guests an elegant atmosphere in which to enjoy the Pacific Northwest's finest Japanese Cuisine. Owner/Chef Tak Suetsugu masterfully prepares the sushi, seafood and steak specialties. Any selection is guaranteed to melt in your mouth and may be complemented with a beverage from their extensive sake, wine and beer menus. Dine at the sushi bar to watch the chef in action, or enjoy your meal in the traditional private tatami rooms.

Nikko has been listed one of America's Top Restaurants by Gourmet Magazine and the Zagat Survey.

Lunch served Monday- Friday. Dinner served Monday- Saturday.

Salmon Kenchin Mushi

PrepTime: 15 minutes
Cooking Time: 15 minutes
Servings Per Recipe: 4

1 **Emerald Sauce:** Puree green peas with 1/3 cup water in a blender. Strain through a fine mesh strainer to remove skins. Place into a sauce pan. Add 1/4 cup dashi, 1/4 teaspoon soy sauce, 1/2 teaspoon salt, and aji-no-moto, to taste. Mix well. Bring to boil over medium heat. Combine 1 teaspoon katakuriko with 1/4 cup water. Add to sauce. Stir well. Strain. Keep warm or cool in refrigerator for later use.

2 **Salmon:** Heat 2 tablespoons salad oil over medium heat in a large sauté pan. Add gobo, carrot, dry onion, shittakes, and konnyaku. Cook until tender, stirring occasionally. Add 3 tablespoons sugar, 1/3 teaspoon salt, 3 tablespoons soy sauce. Mix well until sugar has dissolved. In a separate sauté pan heat 1 tablespoon oil. Add 1 teaspoon sugar and 1 teaspoon soy sauce. Add tofu. Sauté until cooked thoroughly. Combine mushroom mixture and tofu. Sprinkle salmon with salt, not too much. Wrap tofu mixture in salmon. Set in individual serving dishes or a large plate. Steam until ready, about 5 minutes. Pour emerald sauce over. Serve.

Dashi is a Japanese broth. Dashi-no-moto, an instant form of dashi (granulated, powdered, or concentrate) can be found in Asian markets.

1 cup green peas

1/3 cup water

1/4 cup dashi (see Chef Hint)

3 1/2 tablespoons soy sauce

2 teaspoons salt (and as needed)

Aji-no-moto (to taste) optional (Japanese MSG)

1 teaspoon katakuriko (potato starch)

3 tablespoons salad oil

1 gobo, julienned

1 carrot, julienned

1/2 yellow onion, julienned

5 shiitakes, julienned

1/2 konnyaku (yan noodle), par boiled, sliced

3 1/3 tablespoons sugar

7 oz tofu, drained

4 (3-ounce) salmon filets, skinned and boned

Rack of lamb with mint au jus

UNION SQUARE GRILL

SEATTLE'S DOWNTOWN RESTAURANT

621 Union St., Seattle, WA (206)224-4321
(7th & Union)

Union Square Grill is Seattle's quintessential downtown restaurant. Long enjoyed as a favorite meeting place, Union Square Grill is known for its unpretentious style and energetic ambience.

Their contemporary American Cuisine takes on a style of its own. Chef John Broulette's seasonal menus pay special homage to custom dry-aged USDA prime beef grilled over live mesquite hardwood, premium seafood, and locally grown produce. Desserts such as Baked Alaska Flambé are created daily by nationally-recognized pastry chef, Laura Jefferds.

The staff's crisp service is proven by the expert tableside preparations of their Herb Crusted Rack of Lamb and their signature Caesar Salad. The carefully selected wine list features West Coast red wines to complement the menu.

Guests attending Seattle's wide array of downtown entertainment options enjoy the specially-created theater menu.

Herb Crusted Rack of Lamb

PrepTime: 30 minutes
Cooking Time: 15 minutes
Servings Per Recipe: 2

1 teaspoon granulated garlic

1 teaspoon granulated onion

1 3/4 tablespoons kosher salt

1 3/4 teaspoons fresh ground black pepper

4 oz butter, melted

2 tablespoons fresh parsley, chopped

3/4 teaspoon fresh garlic, chopped

1/4 teaspoon fresh rosemary, chopped

3/4 teaspoon shallots, chopped

1 1/2 teaspoons Dijon mustard

1 1/4 cups breadcrumbs

2 tablespoons white wine vinegar

1 tablespoon sugar

1/4 cup au jus (beef broth or liquid au jus)

1/4 cup mint jelly

2 teaspoons cornstarch

2 teaspoons cold water

1 tablespoon fresh mint

2 racks (1 lb each) of lamb, fat cap trimmed 1/8 to 1/4-inch

1/4 cup olive oil

1 **Lamb Rub:** Combine granulated garlic, granulated onion, 1 1/2 tablespoons kosher salt and 1 teaspoon pepper in a bowl. Mix well. Set aside.

2 **Herb Breadcrumbs:** Combine melted butter, parsley, rosemary, garlic, shallots, Dijon, 1/8 teaspoon salt, 3/4 teaspoon black pepper, and breadcrumbs in a bowl. Blend until evenly combined. Set aside.

3 **Mint Au Jus:** Combine vinegar, sugar, au jus, and mint jelly over medium heat in a small sauce pan. Mix well. Bring to a boil. Whisk the cornstarch and cold water together, then slowly whisk into the sauce. Cook until thickened. Remove from heat. Stir in fresh mint. Hold over hot water until ready to use.

4 **Lamb:** Preheat oven to 450° F. Season each rack of lamb with 1 1/2 teaspoons of the lamb rub. Heat 1/4 cup olive oil over high heat in a large sauté pan until hot. Add lamb. Sear lamb until fat is rendered and the meat is seared on all sides. Remove lamb from pan and place onto a baking sheet. Place in oven. Roast for 12 minutes, or to an internal temperature of 120° F, for rare meat. Remove meat from oven and allow to cool until roast can be handled. Pack the fat side of the rack with herb breadcrumbs to a depth of approximately 1/3-inch. Place the rack approximately 6 inches under the broiler. Broil until the crust is crisp and golden brown. Cut the lamb between the bones and serve over a pool of mint au jus.

Sautéed salmon stuffed with pears over risotto and a light sauce

1 Yesler Way, Seattle, WA (206)622-7688

Tucked away in the beautiful historic Pioneer Square, you'll discover what the Seattle locals consider their most precious dining secret: the Al Boccalino Restaurant. Al Boccalino welcomes you with a traditional warmth and elegance that will draw you back again and again.

This is where Chef Donald Alcorn proudly displays his passion for the culinary arts. He introduces a little taste of Italy with specially imported meats and cheeses, then adds the freshest Northwest ingredients to treat you to a celebration of flavors that until now have only been found in the Old Country. From the moment you walk in, you'll realize you've just uncovered a treasure.

Al Boccalino was voted "Best Italian Restaurant" by Seattle Magazine in 1995, 1996 and 1997.

Salmone Ripiene con Pere al Risotto

PrepTime: 15 minutes
Cooking Time: 20 minutes
Servings Per Recipe: 1

3 1/2 tablespoons butter

1 small onion, diced

1 pinch saffron

1/4 cup arborio rice

3 cups chicken stock

Salt and pepper (to taste)

Juice of 1 large lemon

1/2 teaspoon sugar

1/4 cup white wine

1/2 pear, sliced

1 (8-ounce) salmon filet, skinned and boned

Flour (as needed)

1 tablespoon oil

Chives, fresh snipped (to garnish)

1 **Risotto:** Melt 2 tablespoons butter over medium heat in a 1-quart sauce pan. Add onions. Sauté until translucent. Add saffron, arborio rice, and 1 cup chicken stock. Mix well. Cook until stock has absorbed. Add a little more stock and continue the process until all the stock is gone, or rice is cooked. Season with salt and pepper, to taste. Set aside; keep warm.

2 **Sauce:** Combine lemon juice, sugar, white wine, and 1 tablespoon butter over medium heat in a sauté pan. Bring to a simmer; reduce 2 minutes. Set aside; keep warm.

3 **Salmon:** Melt 1 teaspoon butter over medium heat in a small sauté pan. Add pear and sauté until tender. Set aside. Using a sharp knife cut salmon 3/4 the way through, starting in the side of the fish. Stuff the salmon with the pears. Lightly flour the salmon. Heat 1 tablespoon oil over medium-high heat in a large sauté pan. Add salmon and sauté for 3 minutes on each side or until desired temperature is reached.

4 **Serving:** Place risotto on plate. Rest salmon on risotto. Drizzle sauce over salmon. Garnish with chives. Enjoy!

With crispy taro sticks, tropical fruit salsa and a warm ginger rice coulis and cilantro

1900 - 5th Ave., Seattle, WA (206)256-7697
(The Westin Seattle)

Roy's is named for internationally-acclaimed Chef Roy Yamaguchi who founded the restaurant chain several years ago. With over ten locations around the Pacific Rim, each restaurant adds its own geographical influence to the menu.

Roy's Seattle blends French, Italian, Thai, Japanese, Chinese and Polynesian culinary techniques with native Northwest ingredients to create a unique Euro-Asian style. Chef Dean Shinagawa inspires the kitchen as he and his team create dining experiences worth repeating.

Experience taste sensations ranging from Oven Roasted French Toast with Toasted Macadamia Nuts to Roy's Dungeness Crab Cakes, to Alder Broiled Filet Mignon with a Roasted Garlic Cabernet Sauce. Desserts are prepared with the same flair and the famous Melting Hot Chocolate Souffle is a "must try" item. Fish specials often feature the freshest Northwest "catch" making each visit a new experience. Visit soon.

Peppercorn Seared Alaskan Halibut

PrepTime: 60 minutes
Cooking Time: 15 minutes
Servings Per Recipe: 4

2 whole taro roots
Oil (for deep frying)
1/2 bunch cilantro
1 cup salad oil
Salt and white pepper (to taste)
1 mango, peeled and cored, diced small
1 papaya, peeled and seeded, diced small
1/2 sweet onion, diced small
1/2 red bell pepper, cored and seeded, diced small
1/2 bunch cilantro, chopped
1 tablespoon red wine vinegar
1 tablespoon olive oil
4 cups chicken stock
1 tablespoon fresh ginger, chopped
2 cups Niko Calrose rice, cooked
1 1/2 lb fresh Alaskan halibut
2 tablespoons black peppercorns, crushed
Oil for searing fish (to coat pan)
4 bunches baby bok choy
1 teaspoon sesame oil
1 tablespoon Chinese oyster sauce

1 **Taro Sticks:** Remove outer layer of taro root until clean white purplish center is reached. Cut into hand held size and make long thin strips using a kitchen mandolin or use a kitchen knife and julienne cut. Deep fry in hot oil at 375° F until golden brown and reserve on a cloth or paper towel. Season with salt and pepper.

2 **Cilantro Oil:** Blend fresh cilantro and salad oil in blender until cilantro is very fine. Season with salt and white pepper.

3 **Salsa:** In a mixing bowl, add mango, papaya, sweet onion, red bell pepper, chopped cilantro, rice wine vinegar, olive oil, and salt and pepper, to taste. Mix together slightly. Reserve.

4 **Ginger Rice Coulis:** Add chicken stock and fresh ginger to the cooked rice and bring it to a boil until rice is very soft. Then blend the mixture in a blender adding more chicken stock to keep a sauce consistency. Season with salt and white pepper, to taste. (Coulis will be fairly bland - season to taste with more ginger or salt.)

5 **Preparation:** Portion Alaskan halibut to 4 or 5 ounces (using a slight angle so the fish is about 1-inch thick) and reserve. Crush whole black peppercorns using a blender or bottom of a mixing bowl. Gently sprinkle crushed peppercorns on halibut filet and pan sear in an oiled sauté pan over medium heat (about 2 minutes on each side).

6 **Vegetable Bed:** Cut about 1/2 inch off the bottom of the bok choy, so the leaves become loose. Wash baby bok choy and sauté in hot skillet with sesame oil. Add oyster sauce and cook for about 1 minute.

7 **Assembly:** Place cooked baby bok choy in the middle of the plate and top with crispy taro sticks. Top with halibut. Then place the ginger rice coulis around the fish on the plate. Drizzle a little of the cilantro oil on the sauce. Top the halibut with tropical fruit salsa and serve.

A spicy entree with a Pipian Rojo Sauce

Latin Bistro &

Cigar Room

1430 - 34th Ave., Seattle, WA (206)322-5453

The Dulces Latin Bistro is a neighborhood favorite, specializing in Latino Cuisine. Chef Julie Guerrero's interpretation of this cuisine is the fusion of Provencale, Spanish, Italian and regional Mexican flavors. Only the freshest ingredients from the Pacific Northwest are used in her dishes.

Chef Guerrero and her partner Carlos Kainz and Manager Erick Koteles strive to make their guests feel welcome each time they visit. They will assist with wine selections from a list of over 150 different wines. They will gladly take special requests for menu alterations or dietary needs. All this has earned them a Three Star Restaurant rating by the Seattle Tempo.

After dinner guests are invited to the cigar lounge where a great selection of cigars, ports and cognacs are offered. Enjoy flamenco and classical music on Wednesdays and Sundays.

Chiles Rellenos

PrepTime: 15 minutes
Cooking Time: 10 minutes
Servings Per Recipe: 6

1 **Pipian Rojo Sauce:** Heat 1 tablespoon oil over medium heat in a 2-quart nonreactive sauce pan. Add onions. Sauté until transparent. Add tomatoes, tomatillos, garlic and chipolte chiles. Cook for approximately 1 minute. Add chili powder, pumpkin seeds, peanuts, tomato puree, cinnamon, and sugar. Mix well. Season with salt and pepper, to taste. Add water. Leave on medium heat, reduce by half. Place into a blender and puree. Set aside.

2 **Roasting Chiles:** Place each of the Poblano chiles on a high flame. Turning constantly with a pair of tongs, blacken on all sides without cooking the meat of the chiles. Immediately after roasting, place in ice water. Remove the skin of the chile while still in the ice water. Remove chiles; make a slit on the side of each of the chiles, then discard the seeds.

3 **Stuffing:** Divide the two cheeses into 12 equal portions. Combine one portion of each cheese together into an egg shape and stuff each chile, until all remaining chiles are stuffed.

4 **Cooking Chiles:** Roll chiles in flour, then dip into egg and finally into cornmeal. Heat 1/4 cup olive oil over medium heat. Add the chiles, rotating on all sides to sear them. Serve stuffed chiles over Pipian Rojo Sauce. Enjoy.

1 tablespoon + 1/4 cup olive oil

1 1/2 yellow onions, chopped

5 medium tomatoes, chopped

10 tomatillos, chopped

1 clove garlic, minced

2 chipolte chiles in adobo sauce

1/4 cup chili powder

4 oz pumpkin seeds

1/2 cup peanuts, toasted

1/2 cup tomato puree

2 teaspoons cinnamon

2 teaspoons sugar

1 quart water

Salt and pepper (to taste)

12 medium Poblano chiles

1 1/2 cups chèvre cheese

2 cups Monterey Jack cheese, shredded

Flour (as needed)

4 eggs, beaten

1/2 cup cornmeal

A trio of seafood with vegetables with spaghetti noodles tossed in garlic butter

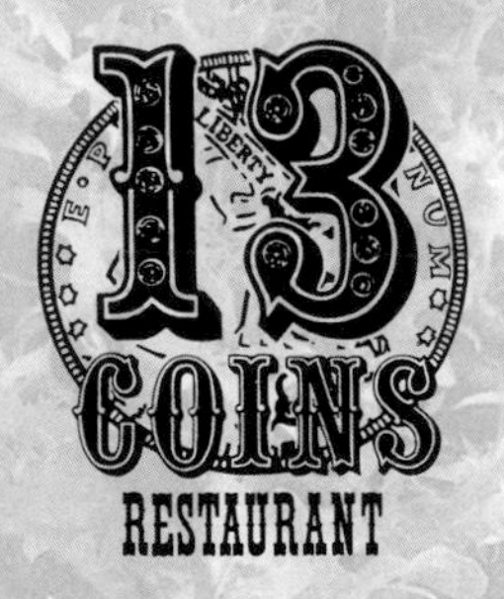

18000 Pacific Hwy. S, Seattle, WA
(206)243-9500

125 Boren N., Seattle, WA
(206)682-2513

Thirteen Coins has served Seattle for over thirty years as the city's favorite 24- hour restaurant. Anything from eggs to steak and lobster is available at any hour of the day, seven days a week.

Private booths and high-backed counter chairs offer a full view of the chefs preparing your food to order. Over 130 items take shape right before your eyes: everything from omelettes flipped in the air to seafood sautéed over flames. Ask for Joe's Special or the Seafood Fettuccine if you want your tastebuds to be pleasantly surprised.

Stop by and you'll discover why Thirteen Coins has been awarded "Best Breakfast in Seattle" and "Best Late Night Dining."

Combination Seafood Sauté

PrepTime: 15 minutes
Cooking Time: 10 minutes
Servings Per Recipe: 2

1 Heat olive oil and garlic over medium heat in a large sauté pan, until garlic sizzles. Add prawns and scallops. Cook for 1 minute, then add halibut. When seafood becomes firm, about 2 minutes, add green pepper, onions, and mushrooms. Season with salt and pepper, to taste. Sauté vegetables until they are al dente. Squeeze in juice of lemon wedges, then drop in wedges. Add tomato wedges and white wine. Sauté for another minute. Then separate ingredients onto two large plates. Turn lemon wedges rind side up. Set aside; keep warm.

2 Place garlic butter in a medium sauté pan. Heat over medium heat until melted. Add cooked pasta. Sauté until hot. (If pasta sticks to pan, add a small amount of water.) Place equal amounts of pasta onto each plate. Top with Parmesan and parsley. Enjoy!

1/4 cup extra virgin olive oil

1/2 teaspoon garlic, chopped

6 jumbo prawns, peeled and deveined

6 large scallops

6 oz halibut, cut into 1 x 1-inch cubes

1 green pepper, cored and seeded, diced into 1-inch squares

1/2 large onion, sliced into 1-inch squares

8 button mushrooms, washed

Salt and pepper (to taste)

1/2 whole lemon, wedged in half, seeds removed

1 tomato (blanched and skinned), sliced in 6 wedges

1/4 cup white wine

2 oz garlic butter

10 oz cooked spaghetti

2 oz Parmesan cheese, grated

Parsley (to garnish)

Hearty Portabella mushrooms with a roasted tomato Dijon sauce

UNION BAY *cafe*

3515 N.E. 45th St., Seattle, WA (206)527-8364

Union Bay Cafe recently moved to a new space, designed by architect George Suyama and beautifully accented by artists Dennis Evans and Nancy Mee. What hasn't changed is the great food, the friendly attitude and the warm atmosphere that originally propelled it to one of the leading neighborhood restaurants in the city.

Chef Mark Manley features the freshest seafood, free-range poultry and game available. Yet his savory vegetarian dishes are also popular items, such as the Portabella Mushrooms shown here. The full flavor and meaty texture of these mushrooms will satisfy even the most committed meat-lover. Union Bay Cafe also offers a wine list of surprising depth, with over a dozen quality wines served by the glass.

Having received Honorable Mention as "Best Neighborhood Restaurant" in Gourmet Magazine 1996, the Union Bay Cafe is one of the must-see places in Seattle. Dinner served Tuesday- Sunday. Reservations recommended.

Grilled Portabella Mushroom "Chops"

PrepTime: 10 minutes
Cooking Time: 20 minutes
Servings Per Recipe: 4

1 tablespoon olive oil (additional, as needed)

2 shallots, diced

2 garlic cloves, minced

2 fresh sage sprigs or 1 tablespoon dry sage

1 tablespoon Dijon mustard

1 tablespoon roasted tomato puree*

1/4 cup port wine (may substitute Madeira, sherry, or Marsala if that is what you have on hand)

2 cups vegetable stock

1 tablespoon unsalted butter

Salt and pepper (to taste)

4 (4-6 oz) Portabella mushrooms

Balsamic vinegar (as needed)

*Coat tomatoes in olive oil and brown well in hot oven. Cool and pass through sieve.

1 **Sauce:** Heat 1 tablespoon olive oil over medium heat in a 1-quart sauce pan. Add shallots and garlic. Sauté until lightly caramelized. Add sage. Sauté briefly. Stir in mustard and tomato puree until emulsified. Add port wine. Reduce by two-thirds. Add vegetable stock. Reduce by three-quarters. Sauce should be slightly thickened. Remove from heat. Stir in butter until melted. Season with salt and pepper, to taste. Set aside; keep warm.

2 **Portabellas:** Slice mushrooms; coat well with olive oil. Season with salt and pepper, to taste, and a splash of balsamic vinegar. These are best grilled on a charbroiler or broiled as close to the element as possible. Turn once and remove when tender. They do not require a lot of cooking. Serve with garlicky mashed potatoes and seasoned vegetables, or your favorite accompaniments.

Tantalizing tender lamb racks with a zesty spinach sauce

CHUTNEYS

CUISINE OF INDIA

519 - 1st Ave. N., Seattle, WA (206)284-6799
605 - 15th Ave. E., Seattle, WA (206)726-1000
1815 N. 45th St., Seattle, WA (206)634-1000

The Chutneys have been in the spotlight ever since they opened their doors. These three affiliated restaurants serve the finest Indian Cuisine in three distinctively different ways. The Queen Anne location offers authentic Indian Cuisine. The Wallingford Center location specializes in a fusion style of cooking, exhibiting a great deal of creativity in its presentations and entrees. And the newest Capital Hill location leans toward the exotic, focusing on seafood and grilled items.

Each continues to receive rave reviews. The Seattle Times Restaurant Critic, John Hinterberger wrote, "The best Indian Restaurant in the city.....I've gone back time and time again." The Chutneys also received the Readers Choice Award by the National Zagat Survey. The survey went on to suggest, "You'll have to try them all and find out which one you like best. The contest will be a fun one."

Visit them all and see for yourself.

Spinach Masala Lamb Rack

PrepTime: 15 minutes
Cooking Time: 25 minutes
Servings Per Recipe: 4

1 **Marinade:** Combine yogurt, 1 tablespoon garlic paste, 1/2 tablespoon ginger paste, 1/2 tablespoon black pepper, 1 teaspoon cumin, and 1 teaspoon coriander powder in a nonreactive container large enough to hold the lamb racks. Season with salt, to taste. Coat the racks in the marinade. Marinate at least 2 hours or over night.

2 **Spinach Sauce:** Heat oil over medium heat in a large sauté pan. Add onions. Sauté until translucent. Add 2 tablespoons coriander, 1 teaspoon cayenne, and 1 teaspoon cumin, one right after the other. Mix well. Cook until browned; stirring all the time. Add spinach; stirring; cook 1 minute. Add 1/2 cup water. Simmer 3-5 minutes. Remove and puree the mixture. Season with salt, to taste. Warm before serving; adding cream to cut down spices, if desired.

3 **Lamb:** Preheat oven to 300° F. Drain racks of marinade. Place on a baking pan. Roast for 25 minutes, or until desired doneness. Slice into individual chops before serving.

4 **Serving:** Place rice in the center of each plate. Pour spinach sauce around the rice. Place lamb around the front of the rice. Garnish with 2 tomato crowns, julienned red peppers and small drops of heavy cream on the spinach sauce.

1 cup plain yogurt

1 1/2 tablespoons garlic paste

1 tablespoon ginger paste

1/2 tablespoon black pepper

2 teaspoons cumin

2 1/2 tablespoons coriander powder

Salt (to taste)

4 (10-ounce) rack of lambs, cleaned and frenched

1 tablespoon oil

1 cup onion, diced

1 teaspoon cayenne pepper

1 cup spinach, cooked

1/2 cup water

Heavy cream (as needed) optional

4 servings rice, cooked (basmati is the best)

4 tomatoes, cut into crowns (to garnish)

1 red bell pepper, seeded and julienned (to garnish)

An array of seafood on top of saffron Arborio rice

2132 - 1st Ave., Seattle, WA
(206)448-8597

Il Gambero means "the prawn" and that's just what Chef/Owner Gaspare Trani specializes in, along with many other seafood specialties. The Italian Cuisine at II Gambero is influenced by Chef Trani's hometown in the Bay of Naples. Yet his new home also inspires him, because he takes full advantage of the bountiful seafood in the Northwest. Bisteccas Florentine and Vitello Osso Buco highlight the menu, as do the halibut and salmon selections.

Chef Trani has a reputation for being one of the hardest-working chefs in Seattle. Each dish is certain to include his subtle nuances.

Warm amber lighting and old brick walls lend a romantic touch to the intimate decor. II Gambero is the place to remember for that special evening.

Risotto Pescatore

PrepTime: 15 minutes
Cooking Time: 25 minutes
Servings Per Recipe: 6

1 **Rice:** Boil rice in water until al dente. Approximately 15 minutes. Set aside.

2 **Seafood:** Heat olive oil over medium-high heat in a large sauté pan. Add garlic, clams, and calamari. Sauté until shells open. Add wine, scallops, crab, prawns, and saffron. Continue to cook until scallops and prawns are thoroughly cooked. Season with salt and pepper, to taste.

3 Remove all of the seafood from the pan. Set aside; keep warm. Add the rice to the pan with juices. Cook over medium heat until rice has absorbed all of the liquid and has turned yellow.

4 Place rice on a large platter. Decorate with seafood. Garnish with parsley. Enjoy.

5 cups Arborio rice

2 tablespoons olive oil

2 cloves garlic, chopped

2 lb manila clams, shells well scrubbed

1/2 lb calamari tubes, cleaned

1/3 cup white wine

8 oz scallops

8 oz Alaskan king crab, shells removed

8 oz fresh prawns, peeled and deveined

2 strands saffron

Salt and pepper (to taste)

Parsley (to garnish)

Grilled salmon on top of soba noodles with a mango papaya salsa

ASIA Grille

2820 - 25th Ave. N.E., Seattle, WA
(206)517-5985

The Asia Grille is the place to go when you're looking for a casual and sophisticated dining experience. This is where you'll discover a spirited interpretation of Asian Cuisine with artistically-prepared and elegantly-presented entrees. They offer a truly unique blend of tastes and textures that you are sure to enjoy, so visit soon and bring your appetite.

Sake Salmon

PrepTime: 85 minutes
Cooking Time: 20 minutes
Servings Per Recipe: 1

1 **Salmon:** Combine lite soy sauce, sake, sugar, ginger, and minced garlic in a nonreactive container. Place salmon into marinade. Cover and refrigerate 1-2 hours.

2 **Salsa:** Combine mangos, papaya, diced red peppers, cilantro, lime juice, and chili sauce in a nonreactive bowl. Mix well. Set aside.

3 **Yakisoba noodles:** Heat a wok with 2 tablespoons oil. Add noodles, red and green bell peppers, onion, and garlic. Toss until heated through. Add soy sauce. Season with salt and pepper, to taste.

4 **Finishing salmon:** Heat a grill. Grill salmon for 1 minute on both sides or until desired doneness (medium to medium rare is recommended).

5 **Serving:** Place noodles on a plate. Place the salmon on noodles. Top the salmon with the salsa. Garnish with rice noodles and scallions.

1 cup lite soy sauce

1 cup sake

2 tablespoons granulated sugar

2 tablespoons fresh ginger, chopped

1 tablespoon garlic, minced

8 ounce salmon filet (fresh King or Atlantic), skinned and boned

1/3 cup mango, diced

1/3 cup papaya, diced

2 tablespoons red pepper, diced

1 tablespoon cilantro, chopped

Juice of 1/2 lime

2 tablespoons sweet chili sauce

2 tablespoons oil

6 oz Yakisoba noodles

2 tablespoons red bell pepper, julienned

2 tablespoons white onion, julienned

2 tablespoons green bell pepper, julienned

1/2 teaspoon fresh garlic, chopped

1/4 cup soy sauce

Salt and pepper (to taste)

Rice noodles (to garnish)

Scallions (to garnish)

With cabernet soy reduction

nishino

3130 E. Madison, Seattle, WA (206)322-5800

When Tatsu Nishino came to the United States thirteen years ago, he dreamed of owning a restaurant. His dream has become a dream-come-true for Seattle sushi lovers. Extensive varieties of seafood are flown in daily ensuring the best selection in the Pacific Northwest and allowing Chef Tatsu Nishino to serve over thirty varieties of sushi.

Yet Chef Nishino refuses to follow one specific cuisine, so on the menu you'll find Baked Dungeness Crab in a Creamy Spicy Sauce, Chilean Sea Bass and Asparagus with Papaya Salsa, and Spicy Garlic Chicken with Shiitake Mushrooms. All dishes are prepared in a simple artistic design, very much in the Japanese tradition.

The open kitchen injects an electricity into the air drawing guests and employees into the enthusiasm. The staff is well-informed and willing to help with any questions you have regarding the menu. An evening at the Nishino Restaurant with its modern Japanese decor will always be a special one.

Toro Steak

PrepTime: 20 minutes
Cooking Time: 25 minutes
Servings Per Recipe: 4

3 tablespoons vegetable oil

1/2 onion, chopped

1 clove garlic, chopped

2 cups Cabernet Sauvigon

1/2 cup Milin (sweet cooking sake)

1 tablespoon soy sauce (plus more, to taste)

1 oz butter

Salt and pepper (to taste)

1 taro root, peeled and sliced paper thin

4 (5-ounce) Toro (fatty tuna, sashimi grade)

1 lb Swiss chard

1 lb shiitake mushrooms

1 tablespoon sake

1 **Sauce:** Heat 1 tablespoon oil over medium-high heat in a 1-quart sauce pan. Add onions and garlic. Sauté until tender. Add red wine. Reduce by half. Strain. Return to pan over medium heat. Add Milin and 1 tablespoon soy sauce. Reduce by half. Stir in butter. Season with salt and pepper, to taste. Set aside; keep warm.

2 **Taro Chips:** Heat a deep fryer with oil. Add taro slices and fry until lightly golden brown. Remove onto paper toweling to remove excess oil. Set aside.

3 **Toro:** Season toro with salt and pepper, to taste. Grill 1-2 minutes on both sides. Keep on a warm plate.

4 **Swiss Chard and Shiitakes:** Heat 2 tablespoons of oil over medium-high heat. Add Swiss chard and shiitakes. Cook until tender. Season with 1 tablespoon sake and soy sauce, to taste. Adjust seasoning with salt and pepper, to taste, if necessary.

5 **Finishing:** Equally place chard and shiitake in center of plates. Slice each toro and place onto chard. Ladle sauce over toro. Garnish with fried taro chips. Serve. Enjoy!

Spicy grilled marinated pork chops with jalapeño preserves

PARAGON

RESTAURANT · BAR

FUN DINING · PLUSH BOOTHS · GENEROUS COCKTAILS

2125 Queen Anne Ave. N., Seattle, WA
(206)283-4548

Located atop the picturesque Queen Anne Hill, Paragon Bar & Grill invites you into a decor of contemporary artistry mixed with nostalgia. Sink into a plush booth near the roaring fireplace or position yourself next to one of the metal sculptures whimsically placed throughout the restaurant.

Chef Christopher Cunio continues this eclectic feel in his cuisine, stirring up a menu that reflects the restaurant's Pacific Rim location. Choose your meal from the seasonal specials or from the chef's nightly featured entrees. Their wine list showcases the best of California and Northwest wines.

Accolades for the Paragon are regional and national. The Seattle Times wrote, "Paragon's the place for food, jazz, people." People Magazine concurs. Visit the Paragon soon and see if you agree.

Marinated Pork Rib Chops

PrepTime: 35 minutes
Cooking Time: 60 minutes
Servings Per Recipe: 8

1 **Chili Marinade:** Combine the hoisin, soy sauce, 1 cup sugar, sambal, ginger, garlic, and green onions in a nonreactive container large enough to hold the pork. Submerge the rib chops in the marinade. Marinate in refrigerator for 24 hours.

2 **Jalapeño preserves:** Heat vinegar and 2 cups sugar over medium heat in a 1-quart saucepan. Heat until sugar dissolves. Add jalapeños and simmer 3 minutes. Mix cornstarch and pectin. Whisk into sauce. Add bell peppers. Simmer 5 minutes. Pull off heat. Add pears. Mix well. Set in cooler.

3 **Ribs:** Preheat a grill. Remove chops from marinade. Place on grill. Cook for 5 minutes on each side. Cook until desired temperature is reached. Remove from grill and serve with jalapeño preserves.

1 cup hoisin

1 cup soy sauce

3 cups sugar

1/2 cup sambal (a condiment found in Asian markets)

1 tablespoon fresh ginger, chopped

1 teaspoon garlic, chopped

2 stalks green onions, chopped

8 (8-ounce) pork rib chops

3/4 cup apple cider vinegar

1/2 cup jalapeños, seeded and sliced

1 1/2 tablespoons cornstarch

6 oz fruit pectin

1 cup red bell peppers, sliced

1 cup Asian pears, diced

Tender herb crusted chicken accompanied by a rich Dijon cream sauce

FIGARO Bistro

11 Roy St., Seattle, WA (206)284-6465

The Figaro Bistro offers a pan-French experience by taking the best culinary inspirations from many regions. Owners Maitre d' Phillippe Bollache and Chef Laurent Gabrel grew up in France where these flavors were second nature to them. It is their intent to share these wonderful flavors with you, as prepared by Chef Adam Hoffman.

One of their signature entrees is Steak Frite, tender slices of garlic-and-herb-marinated beef that will melt in your mouth. Another entree favorite is the Roasted Pork Loin with Spinach-and-Gruyère Stuffing in a Demi-Glacé. If you like an authentic Bouillabaisse, Figaro's is the best in town. The wine list is an assembly of moderately priced labels from France and the United States.

From their Onion Soup to their Crème Brûlée, the Figaro Bistro offers the best of France.

Supreme de Volaille

PrepTime: 20 minutes
Cooking Time: 25 minutes
Servings Per Recipe: 4

1 **Sauce:** Heat stock over medium heat in a small sauce pan. Bring to a simmer; reduce to 1 tablespoon. Melt 1 tablespoon of butter over medium heat in a small saucepan. Add shallots. Sauté until translucent. Add 1 tablespoon whole grain mustard, reduced duck stock, and heavy cream. Reduce until sauce coats the back of a spoon. Season with salt and white pepper, to taste.

2 **Chicken:** Preheat oven to 425° F. Soak breadcrumbs in melted butter. Rub each chicken breast with 1/2 tablespoon of whole grain mustard. Season with salt and black pepper, to taste. Place onto a sided baking pan. Sprinkle with chopped sage, thyme, oregano, rosemary, and soaked breadcrumbs. Bake for 10 minutes or until done. Serve with sauce. Enjoy!

1 cup (8-ounce) duck stock

1 tablespoon butter

1/2 teaspoon shallots

3 tablespoons whole grain mustard

1/2 cup heavy cream

Salt and white pepper (to taste)

1/2 cup breadcrumbs

3 tablespoons butter, melted

4 (6-ounce) chicken breast, wing bone in (frenched)

Black pepper (to taste)

1 tablespoon sage, chopped

1/2 teaspoon thyme, chopped

1 teaspoon oregano

1 1/2 teaspoons rosemary

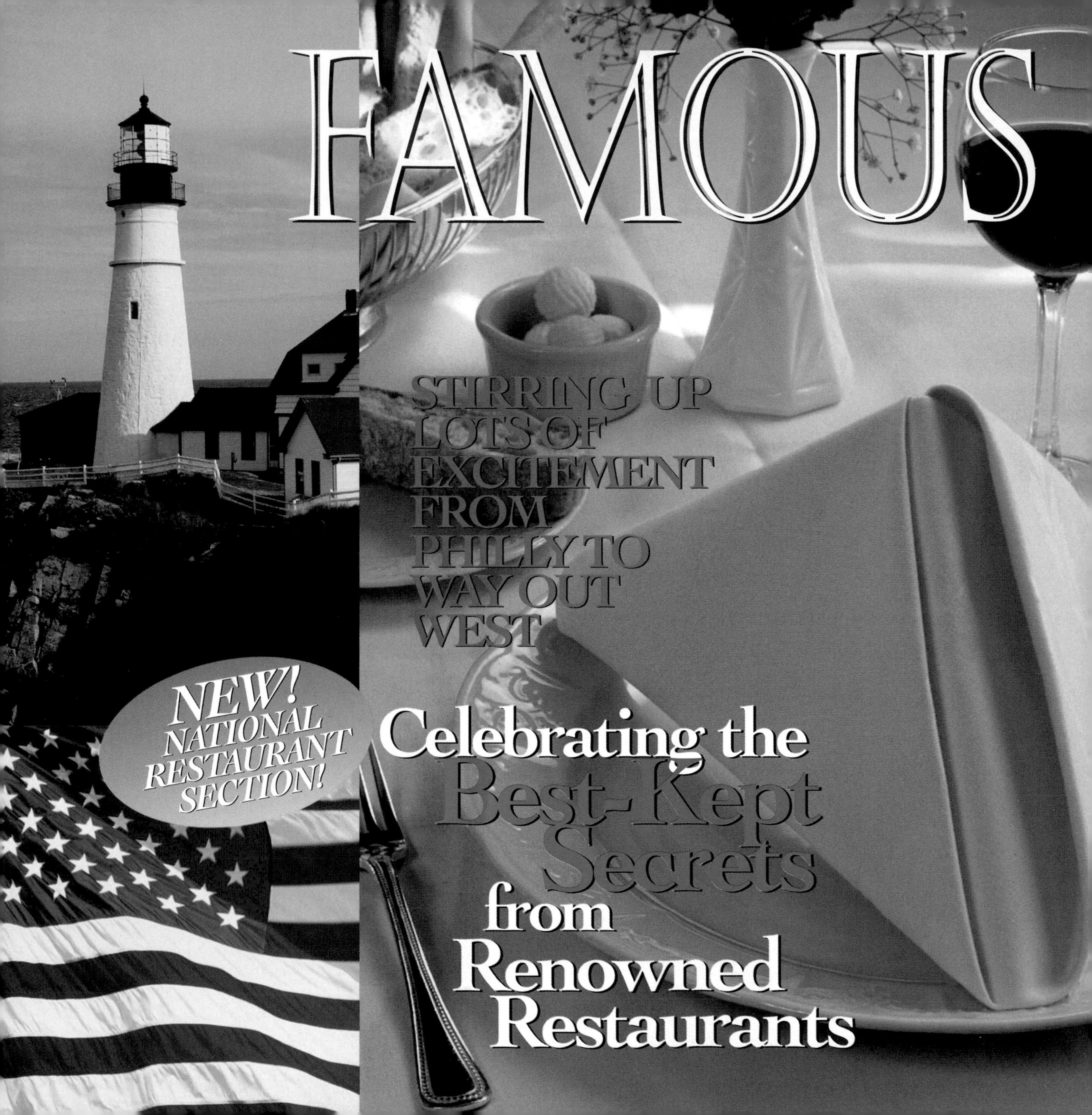
FAMOUS
STIRRING UP LOTS OF EXCITEMENT FROM PHILLY TO WAY OUT WEST
NEW! NATIONAL RESTAURANT SECTION!
Celebrating the Best-Kept Secrets from Renowned Restaurants

SECRETS

RECIPES ONLY INSIDERS KNEW (UNTIL NOW!)

Bringing our long awaited TASTE-OF-THE-TOWN RECIPES into your very own kitchen

Signature crab cake with light mustard sauce accompanied by a small green salad

1523 Walnut St., Philadelphia, PA (215)567-1000

Le Bec Fin has been a restaurant for memorable dining experiences since 1970. In 28 years, Chef/Owner Georges Perrier has made it an institution and a tradition.

Le Bec Fin offers a phenomenal six-course menu with a continuous stream of superlative dishes. Every detail is important to Chef Perrier. His dining room staff delivers impeccable service with an unusual blend of French ritual with American informality.

The hospitality industry regularly gives Le Bec Fin its highest accolades.

"5 Stars" - Mobil Travel Guide

"AAA Five Diamond Award"

Country's Highest Scoring Restaurant - Zagat

Philadelphia's "Top Table" - Gourmet Magazine

"#1 Restaurant in the Nation" - Conde Nast Traveler Magazine

"1989 Chef of the Year" - Maitres Cuisiniers de France

Galette de Crabe "Le Bec-Fin"

PrepTime: 60 minutes
Cooking Time: 15 minutes
Servings Per Recipe: 8-10

For the Galettes:

14 oz large shrimp, peeled and deveined

1 bunch scallions, trimmed and sliced into thin rings

4 tablespoons butter (divided)

2 whole eggs, cold

2 cups heavy cream, icy cold

4 tablespoons Dijon mustard

1 tablespoon Worcestershire Sauce

1 tablespoon Tabasco Sauce

1 pound jumbo crabmeat, picked through removing any shell or cartilage

Olive oil (as needed)

For the Sauce:

1 egg yolk

1 tablespoon sherry vinegar

2 tablespoons Dijon mustard

1/2 cup chicken stock

1 1/2 cups olive oil

2 tablespoons whole-grain mustard

Salt and pepper (to taste)

For the Endive:

1 tablespoon butter

2 teaspoons lemon juice, fresh

3 heads Belgian endive, cored and cut into 1-inch lengths

1 teaspoon sugar

Salt and ground white pepper (to taste)

1 lb haricot verts (slender young green beans) trimmed and blanched (optional)

Additional Equipment:

4-5 (3-inch) ring molds

1 **Galettes:** Chill shrimp, bowl and steel "s" blade of a food processor, in the freezer for 30 minutes.

2 In a small skillet, sauté the scallions in 1 tablespoon of butter, until just wilted. Set aside to cool.

3 Place shrimp in food processor bowl fitted with the "s" blade, and puree on high speed for 1 minute or until well chopped. Using a rubber spatula, scrape down sides of bowl; add eggs and process until mixture appears smooth and shiny (about 2 minutes). With machine running, slowly pour in heavy cream. Scrape bowl and process again until cream is incorporated. Transfer shrimp mixture to a bowl; stir in mustard, Worcestershire, and Tabasco. Gently fold in cooked scallions and crab meat.

4 Place 4 or 5 (3-inch) oiled ring molds into a lightly oiled non-stick pan; fill each ring with the mixture - smoothing off the tops with a spoon. Over medium heat, cook crab cakes until golden brown (about 2 minutes on each side). Once the cakes are browned, push down rings to cut off any excess crab mixture; remove rings from around crab cakes. Remove cakes from pan. Repeat procedure until all crab mixture is used.

5 **Sauce:** In a blender or food processor, combine egg yolk, vinegar, Dijon, and chicken stock. Blend until smooth (about 30 seconds). While machine is running, drizzle in olive oil until the sauce is emulsified (creamy in appearance). Add mustard and season with salt and pepper to taste.

6 **Endive:** In a small sauté pan, heat butter and lemon juice. Add endive and sugar; toss together. Cook over medium heat until endive is wilted (but not soft) and pan juices are absorbed. Season with salt and pepper to taste, and set aside.

7 **Putting it together:** Preheat oven to 400° F. Place the crab cakes on a buttered nonstick baking pan and bake for 5 minutes or until cakes are springy to the touch. In a small pot, slowly heat the sauce over low heat - do not let it boil. Place a small amount of endive onto each plate, top with 1 or 2 crab cakes. Ladle sauce over cakes and serve immediately.

If in need of a ring mold - for small crab cakes use a round biscuit cutter, for a large one, use cleaned empty tuna can. Browned crab cakes can be refrigerated and reheated (up to 1 day).

Layered potato pancakes, minced egg, smoked salmon, horseradish crème fraîche and caviar

A Q U A

252 California St., San Francisco, CA
(415)956-9662

Aqua operates out of a magnificent post-1906 earthquake building in the heart of San Francisco's bustling Financial District. Owner Charles Condy and Executive Chef Michael Mina join forces to redefine seafood dining with their elegant tribute to the flavors of the sea. Chef Mina's intensely flavorful and creative seafood cooking has earned him a reputation as one of the nation's most influential and respected chefs.

Aqua is a model for the contemporary American restaurant design, effortlessly combining a relaxed yet elegant ambiance. Through the soaring glass doors trimmed in white maple, Charles Condy's dramatic California landscape springs to life. A series of small frescoes, by notable Bay area artist Wade Hoefer, chronicle the sun's movement over the Pacific from sunrise to sunset. At the rear of the dining area there is a large fresco depicting a rosy sun dipping past the horizon of a quiet lake - a fitting conclusion to a perfect meal.

"1997 Rising Star Chef of the Year Award" - James Beard Foundation

Caviar Parfait Tasting

PrepTime: 30 minutes
Cooking Time: 5 minutes
Servings Per Recipe: 10

1 **Potato Cakes:** Bake potatoes in 375° F oven until tender (approximately 30 minutes).

2 Grate potatoes using a hand grater. In a bowl, mix together potatoes, herbs, egg whites, salt and potato starch; mix ingredients well. Shape cakes into 2 1/2-inch diameter mold. If potato cakes are not moist enough to stick, add additional egg white.

3 In a large deep pot, add oil and heat. When oil is hot, deep fry potato cakes at 350° F until golden brown. Remove cakes to paper towels to drain, set aside momentarily.

4 **Egg Mixture:** Separate yolks and white of hard-boiled eggs and sift through a small strainer. Add parsley and minced red onion; season mixture with salt and pepper. Separate 5 tablespoons for garnish.

5 **Horseradish Crème Frâiche:** In a bowl, mix together, crème frâiche, horseradish, lemon zest, and chives; season with salt and pepper. Whip mixture until stiff.

6 **Dill Oil:** In a blender or food processor, process dill and oil; season to taste with salt and pepper.

7 **Putting it Together:** On a medium dinner plate, place potato cake in center. Using a ring mold, layer on top of potato cake - first - egg mixture, second - diced salmon, third - horseradish crème frâiche, and the top - caviar.

8 Garnish plate with remaining egg mixture and dill oil.

Ring molds can be purchased at specialty kitchen shops.

For the Potato Cake:

4 russet potatoes, scrubbed

1/2 cup fines herbes (thyme, chervil, chives and parsley)

2 egg whites

2 tablespoons salt

2 tablespoons potato starch

Vegetable oil

For the Egg Mixture:

7 eggs, hard-boiled

2 teaspoons parsley, trimmed and chopped

2 teaspoons red onion, peeled and minced

Salt and pepper (to taste)

For the Horseradish Crème Frâiche:

1 1/2 cups crème frâiche

1 teaspoon horseradish

2 teaspoons lemon zest, chopped

2 teaspoons chives, chopped

Salt and pepper (to taste)

For the Dill Oil:

1/2 bunch dill, blanched

1/2 cup canola oil

For the Caviar and Smoked Salmon:

10 oz osetra caviar

2 cups smoked salmon, diced

Huge mushrooms filled with squash puree, wrapped in phyllo & topped with Balsamic Syrup

RAM'S HEAD INN

Country Cozy Dining

9 West White Horse Pike, Absecon, NJ
(609)652-1700

Ram's Head Inn is a beautiful restaurant set on five country acres with sprawling gardens and flower-lined fences. Just eight miles from the bustling Atlantic City casinos, its wood-burning fireplaces and soft candlelight provide a respite for the senses and enhance the dining rooms.

Guests at Ram's Head Inn have a chance to enjoy quiet, distinctive country dining in an elegant and cozy atmosphere. Cocktails and other beverages can be enjoyed in the Gallery or in the Tavern by the fireplace.

Executive Chef Luigi Baretto has trained and worked throughout Europe.

AAA Four Diamond Award

DiRoNA Award

Phyllo Purse of Portabella Mushrooms

PrepTime: 60 minutes
Cooking Time: 70 minutes
Servings Per Recipe: 1-4

1 **Squash Puree:** Preheat oven to 400° F. Cut squash lengthwise in half; remove seeds. Place cut side down on an oiled baking sheet. Roast in oven for 1 hour, or until tender. Remove outer shell; in a food processor, puree pulp with butter. Season with salt, pepper, and nutmeg, to taste. Fold in almonds and set aside.

2 **Mushrooms:** In a nonreactive container, add 1/2 cup olive oil, garlic, parsley, salt, and pepper. Coat the mushrooms in the marinade; let mushrooms marinate for 30 minutes. Lower oven temperature to 350° F, place marinated mushrooms in an oven-proof dish; roast in oven until tender, approximately 10-15 minutes.

3 **Balsamic Reduction:** In a saucepot, combine balsamic vinegar and port wine. Bring to a simmer and reduce to 1 cup or until syrupy consistency is reached (approximately 20 minutes). Adjust seasonings with salt and pepper, to taste.

4 **Putting it Together:** Generously spread butternut squash puree onto stem side of mushrooms. Lay one sheet of phyllo onto a clean surface. Brush with melted butter. Lay the second sheet of phyllo on top and brush again with butter; top with last sheet of phyllo. Divide sheets into 4 equal squares. Place filled mushroom caps atop each square. Fold phyllo dough to encase mushroom to form into a purse. Place on a baking sheet and bake at 350° F for 10 minutes (or until golden brown). Paint plate with balsamic syrup (reduction) and top with mushrooms. Garnish with julienned peppers and serve.

For the Squash:

1 butternut squash

Salt and pepper (to taste)

Nutmeg (to taste)

4 tablespoons butter

2 tablespoons toasted sliced almonds

For the Mushrooms:

1/2 cup olive oil

Salt and pepper (to taste)

1 tablespoon garlic, chopped

1 teaspoon parsley, chopped

4 medium to large Portabella mushrooms, cleaned

For the Balsamic Reduction:

3 cups balsamic vinegar

1 cup port wine

For the Phyllo:

3 sheets phyllo dough

8 tablespoons butter, melted

For the Garnish:

1/2 red pepper, seeded, deveined and cut into fine julienne

1/2 green pepper, seeded, deveined and cut into fine julienne

1/2 yellow pepper, seeded, deveined and cut into fine julienne

An appetizer with an Asian flair - seafood potstickers with sake dip and hot mustard sauce

dahlia lounge

1904 - 4th Ave., Seattle, WA (206)682-4142

A visit to Seattle wouldn't be complete without a visit to the Dahlia Lounge, Chef Tom Douglas' stylish and inventive restaurant.

Located in the heart of the city, the award-winning Dahlia Lounge serves the finest in Northwest cuisine. Chef Douglas and his talented kitchen crew bring imaginative specialties to your table in a setting that is whimsical, warm and inviting. Please visit their website. (www.tomdouglas.com)

"Seattle's Quintessential and Most Creative Restaurant" - Food and Wine Magazine

Lobster and Shiitake Potstickers

PrepTime: 60 minutes
Cooking Time: 10 minutes
Servings Per Recipe: 6-8

For the Pot Stickers:

2/3 lb raw lobster meat

1/3 lb raw shrimp meat

1 1/2 cups shiitake mushrooms, cleaned and thinly sliced

1/3 cup carrots, peeled and finely diced

1 tablespoon toasted sesame seeds

1 tablespoon green onion, trimmed and very finely chopped

1 tablespoon cilantro, finely chopped

1/2 teaspoon garlic, peeled and minced

2 teaspoons Chinese garlic-chili paste

40 wonton or gyoza wrappers

Peanut or vegetable oil for (sautéing)

For the Sake Dip:

1/2 cup sake

1/4 cup soy sauce

1/4 cup rice wine vinegar

1 small serrano chili, seeded and chopped

1/4 teaspoon minced garlic

1/4 teaspoon fresh ginger, peeled and minced

1 tablespoon sugar

1 tablespoon green onion, finely chopped

For the Hot Mustard:

1/4 cup dry hot mustard

1/3 cup water, or as needed

2 tablespoons soy sauce

2 tablespoons rice wine vinegar

2 teaspoons honey

1 teaspoon sesame oil

1 tablespoon toasted sesame seeds

1 Puree lobster and shrimp meat in food processor until smooth. In a skillet, sauté shiitake mushrooms and carrots in a little of the peanut oil until softened; allow to cool. In a large mixing bowl, combine pureed lobster and shrimp, sautéed shiitakes and carrots, sesame seeds, green onion, cilantro, garlic, and garlic-chili paste. Mix thoroughly.

2 To form potstickers, lay a wrapper down on wax paper. Wet the edges of the wrapper with an index finger dipped in water. Place one tablespoon of the filling in the center of the wrapper and bring two opposing points of the wrapper together to form a triangle. Press the edges together, making a series of small creases along the edges. Refrigerate until all potstickers are assembled.

3 In a large pot, bring 1 gallon of water to boil over high heat. Add potstickers, a few dozen at a time, and cook for 5-8 minutes. When ready, they should float to the surface of the water. Using a small sieve or mesh skimmer, gently scoop potstickers out of the water, being careful not to break them. Continue until all potstickers are poached.

4 Heat about 2 tablespoons of oil in a 10-inch non-stick sauté pan over medium heat. Pan-fry the potstickers in batches (no more than 10 at a time), browning on both sides. Keep warm until all potstickers have been pan-fried, using more oil as needed.

5 **Sake Dip:** In a small pan, combine sake, soy sauce, vinegar, chili, garlic, ginger, and sugar. Warm gently until sugar has dissolved. Remove from heat, cool, then add green onion.

6 **Hot Mustard:** In a small bowl, combine dry mustard with water to form a paste. Mix in soy sauce, rice wine vinegar, honey, sesame oil, and sesame seeds. Add more water if needed to make a nice dipping consistency.

7 **Putting it Together:** Serve potstickers with lime wedges, sake dip, and hot mustard.

Crisp chilled shrimp accompanied by a zesty Asian-flavored shrimp sauce

the Tillerman

2245 E. Flamingo, Las Vegas, NV (702)731-4024

For 20 years, The Tillerman has been known as Home of the Freshest Seafood in Las Vegas - Select Alaskan King Crab Legs, Australian Lobster Tails and Maine Lobster with Angel Hair Pasta, to name just a few of their offerings. Their menu also features delicious steak, chicken and lamb dishes.

The Tillerman's large Garden Room is filled with live ficus trees, plants and an incredible retractable skylight that opens to expose the brilliance of the stars in the night sky.

Timeless comfort, a unique atmosphere, great service and an award-winning wine list, The Tillerman is sure to make your evening a night to remember.

"Top 5 Restaurants-1998" - Wine Spectator

"Best Seafood Restaurant-1998" - Las Vegas Review Journal

Asian Shrimp Cocktail

PrepTime: 10 minutes
Cooking Time: 6 minutes
Servings Per Recipe: 4

1 **Sauce:** In a mixing bowl, combine with a whisk - dry mustard, and vinegar. Add the soy sauce, honey, ginger, garlic, both oils, and green onion; combine well and chill.

2 **Shrimp:** In a large pot, combine water, onion, peppercorns, and bay leaves; bring to a boil.

3 Add shrimp to water and cook until they are firm and appear orange in color. Strain in a colander and cover them in ice to stop the cooking process. Once cool, peel shrimp and run a sharp knife down the back to devein them. Chill to very cold.

4 **Putting it Together:** Place napa cabbage on plate, top with chilled shrimp and serve with a side cup of sauce. Garnish with a lime wedge and a cilantro sprig.

For the Sauce:

1/3 cup dry mustard

1/3 cup rice wine vinegar

1/2 cup soy sauce

1/2 cup honey

1 tablespoon fresh ginger, peeled and finely grated

1 teaspoon fresh garlic, peeled and finely chopped

1/3 cup sesame oil

1 3/4 cup peanut oil

1/8 cup green onions, thinly sliced

For the Shrimp:

1 gallon water

1 small yellow onion peeled

1 tablespoon black peppercorns

2 bay leaves

20 large raw shrimp (shelled)

Garnish:

Napa cabbage

Lime wedge(s)

Cilantro Sprigs

Wild and flavorful - this mushroom soup is the perfect first course or light entrée

CENTRAL PARK AT WEST 67TH ST.,
NEW YORK, NY (212)873-3200

Tavern on the Green is a grand café overlooking Central Park. It is a genuine showstopper, overflowing with crystal chandeliers, hand-carved mirrors and stained glass. Critics say, "If Oz had a restaurant, this would be it!"

Tavern on the Green is open seven days a week, 365 days a year. Located on New York's Upper West Side, it is just three blocks from Lincoln Center and a quick cab ride to Carnegie Hall and Broadway.

Constructed to house sheep in 1870, the building became a restaurant in 1934. In 1974, Warner LeRoy, who revolutionized the American dining scene with his legendary Maxwell's Plum, took over the restaurant and embarked upon a $10 million renovation, which became Tavern on the Green.

From the moment it opened on August 31, 1976, the reinvigorated Tavern took New York by storm, dazzling the city with its decorative setting, eclectic menus and all-around playfulness.

Sam Hazen's Harvest Wild Mushroom Soup

PrepTime: 15 minutes
Cooking Time: 45 minutes
Servings Per Recipe: 4

2 cups shiitake mushrooms, cleaned and stemmed (stems reserved)

2 cups Portobello mushrooms, cleaned and stemmed (stems and gills reserved)

4 cups crimini mushrooms, cleaned, stemmed (stems reserved) and sliced

1 cup domestic mushrooms, cleaned and sliced (stems reserved)

2 large onions, peeled and sliced

2 heads of fennel (tops reserved), sliced

1/2 stick unsalted butter (for sautéeing)

2 whole russet potatoes, peeled

1 quart chicken broth (homemade or prepared)

1 bunch fresh thyme

1/4 cup garlic, peeled and chopped

Salt and pepper (as needed)

Truffle oil (to garnish)

Porcini powder (to garnish)

1 Slice and stem all domestic and criminis; reserve the stems, slice fennel. Reserve tops of fennel. Slice onion.

2 In a heavy bottom pot, gently sauté onions, fennel, domestic and crimini mushrooms in unsalted butter. Do not brown mixture until fennel is tender.

3 During this time (in a bowl), toss shiitakes and Portobellos in oil, thyme, salt, pepper, and chopped garlic. Lay out on baking sheets and roast in 350° F oven until golden brown.

4 In a pot, place reserved mushroom stems and fennel tops in chicken broth and allow to infuse over medium heat, then remove.

5 Remove baking sheet from oven; discard thyme and garlic. Place browned mushrooms into soup pot; add potatoes after slicing thin. At this point, all mushrooms, fennel slices, and onions should be in one pot. Add broth. Simmer until potato is fully cooked.

6 Remove soup from heat source and purée in blender or food processor (process in small batches). Adjust seasoning with salt and pepper. Finish soup with truffle oil and porcini powder.

Truffle oil and porcini powder can be purchased at specialty food shops.

Pear salad with tiny beans, rice wine vinaigrette, honey crusted almonds and scallops

1 Athenaeum St., Cambridge, MA (617)225-2121

A renovated Cambridge ink factory is the backdrop for Chef/Owner Stan Frankenthaler's innovative Asian-tinged cuisine. Since its opening, only three short years ago, Salamander has been recognized by every major publication in the country; the Boston Globe proclaimed it "a four-star restaurant in the making." As soon as you enter the gracious dining room with exposed kitchen, the aromas of the wood-burning hearth excite your senses. The restaurant showcases works by local artists, as well as fruits, produce, and cheeses grown and produced locally. The chef's signature dish of lightly fried lobster with lemongrass, ginger and Thai basil highlights the ever-changing menu of seasonal specialties available. Two private rooms, an attentive/knowledgeable staff, and an award-winning wine list are all part of why Travel and Leisure says this is "the one not to miss". Just minutes from downtown Boston, Salamander is decidedly worth seeking out. Reservations are recommended, walk-ins always welcomed.

Asian Pear Salad with Pear Glazed Scallops

PrepTime: 20 minutes
Cooking Time: 10 minutes
Servings Per Recipe: 4

1 **Salad:** In a pot of boiling water, blanch the haricot vert and reserve. Wash all greens well; trim and cut frisée in half and reserve along with the haricot vert, peppers and pears.

2 **Vinaigrette:** In a bowl, whisk together shallots, ginger, rice vinegar, mirin, pear nectar, both oils, salt and pepper.

3 **Almonds:** In a sauce pan, caramelize honey; add in coriander and chili flakes - then stir in almonds. Remove from heat, quickly separate almonds onto an oiled baking sheet (to avoid clumping); allow almonds to cool.

4 **Scallops:** Clean the scallops and reserve. Prepare the glaze - in a small sauce pan, combine sugar, water, ginger, and pickling spice; reduce to a thick syrup and strain into pear nectar.

5 **Putting it Together:** In one sauté pan, season and sear the frisée; toss in remaining greens, haricot vert, peppers and the vinaigrette. Season with salt and pepper, toss and remove to serving plates. In a second sauté pan (heat to hot), season and sear the scallops; glaze them and arrange on salad.

6 Garnish with honey-spice almonds and serve.

For the Salad:
1/4 pound haricot vert (slender young green beans)
1 sweet red pepper, seeded, deveined and julienned
4 small heads frisée (a variety of endive)
1/4 pound mizuna
1/4 pound baby spinach, washed well and trimmed
1 head radicchio
2 Asian pears (other varieties may be substituted) and julienned

For the Vinaigrette:
1 shallot, peeled and minced
1 tablespoon ginger, peeled and minced
3 tablespoons rice vinegar
1 tablespoon mirin (sweet rice wine)
2 tablespoons pear nectar
2 tablespoons sesame oil
1/4 cup canola oil
Salt and pepper (to taste)

For the Almonds:
1/2 cup honey
1 teaspoon ground coriander
1 teaspoon ground chili flakes
1 cup toasted whole almonds

For the Scallops:
8-12 ounces pristine scallops
1/4 cup sugar
1/4 cup water
1 slice fresh ginger (peeled)
1 tablespoons pickling spice
1/4 cup pear nectar
Salt and pepper (to taste)

Beef filet grilled to perfection and topped with a red wine sauce & a horseradish sauce

417 Royal St., New Orleans, LA (504)525-9711

Dining out in New Orleans would not be complete without a visit to the world famous Brennan's Restaurant. Breakfast at Brennan's is a tradition for local New Orleanians and visitors from all parts of the globe. Brennan's is also recognized for its outstanding lunches and dinners.

Founded by Owen Jr., Jimmy and Ted Brennan, the restaurant is located in the historic Murphy House, a pink stucco mansion at 417 Royal Street in the heart of the French Quarter. Brennan's is noted for its lush courtyard and elegant intimate dining rooms - 12 in all.

Southern hospitality is dispensed at Brennan's on a grand scale and Brennan's 50,000-bottle wine cellar has been repeatedly recognized by the Wine Spectator as one of the most outstanding in the world.

"Grand Award" - Wine Spectator

Travel Holiday Magazine Dining Award yearly since 1956

"Top Five Restaurants of New Orleans" - Zagat Survey

Filet Stanley

PrepTime: 15-20 minutes
Cooking Time: 10-15 minutes
Servings Per Recipe: 8

1 **Brennan's Red Wine Mushroom Sauce:** In a large saucepan or Dutch oven, melt the butter. Add onion and sauté for several minutes, until tender. Stir in the tomato paste, mushrooms and paprika. Cook until the mushrooms are tender; add the flour. Stir the mixture until well blended, then using a whisk, incorporate the beef stock. When sauce is smooth, add scallions, Worcestershire, wine, and garlic. Season with salt and pepper to taste. Simmer about 25 minutes, serve warm with steaks.

2 **Horseradish Sauce:** In a saucepan, combine cream, pepper, and salt. Cook over medium heat (do not let the cream reach a boil). Blend the butter and flour together, and form a small ball. Add butter ball to the simmering cream. Cook until sauce is smooth; add horseradish. Serve warm with steaks.

3 **Filet Stanley:** Prepare a grill or broiler. Sprinkle the halved steaks on both sides with salt and pepper. Grill or broil meat to desired doneness.

4 In a large skillet, melt butter and sauté sliced bananas until tender and lightly browned (approximately 4 minutes per side).

5 **Putting it Together:** Place 2 Holland rusks in the center of 8 heated plates. Arrange a slice of banana on either side of the rusks (near edge of plate). Spoon horseradish sauce between the bananas and the rusks. Place a cooked filet on each Holland rusk and top with Brennan's Red Wine Mushroom Sauce.

Suggested accompaniments: fresh baked french bread & butter, Cabernet Sauvignon.

For the Brennan's Red Wine and Mushroom Sauce: Yields 3 cups

1/2 cup butter (1 stick)
1 cup onion, peeled and diced
1/2 cup tomato paste
2 cups sliced mushrooms
1 1/2 tablespoons paprika
1/4 cup all-purpose flour
3 cups beef stock (homemade or prepared)
2 cups scallions, trimmed and sliced
1 tablespoon Worcestershire Sauce
3/4 cup Burgundy wine
1 tablespoon minced garlic
Salt and pepper (to taste)

For the Horseradish Sauce: Yields 1 1/2 cups

2 cups heavy cream
1/4 teaspoon white pepper
1/4 teaspoon salt
1/4 teaspoon butter
2 tablespoons all-purpose flour
2 tablespoons horseradish

For the Filet Stanley:

8 beef filets, (8-ounces each), halved
Salt and freshly ground black pepper (to taste)
1/2 cup butter
8 bananas, peeled and sliced in half lengthwise
16 Holland rusks (Zwieback toast-like bread)
1/2 cup horseradish sauce (see recipe)
2 cups Brennan's Red Wine and Mushroom Sauce (see recipe)

A unique appetizer with an Asian flair

THE FOUR SEASONS

99 E. 52nd St., New York, NY (212)754-9494

Not to be confused with the hotel chain with a similar name, The Four Seasons is a world-class restaurant designed in 1959 by Phillip Johnson, one of this century's finest architects.

Located in the Seagram Building on Park Avenue, The Four Seasons is one of the city's most glamourous restaurants. During lunch it plays host to movers and shakers in the worlds of politics, finance, and publishing. When the lights go down, the restaurant becomes an irresistably romantic place to enjoy the most delicious wines and foods, like the Crisp Nori Tuna with Blood Orange Miso Sauce pictured here.

Crisp Nori Tuna with Blood Orange Miso Sauce

PrepTime: 10 minutes
Cooking Time: 10 minutes
Servings Per Recipe: 2

1 **Tuna:** Clean and trim tuna into cylindrical shape. Spread wasabi paste on tuna to season.

2 Lay out nori wrapper and put on julienned vegetables, top with tuna and roll (like sushi); seal with tempura flour mix.

3 Dip tuna into tempura flour mix until well coated; roll tuna into panko crumbs until well coated.

4 **Sauce:** In a sauce pan, reduce orange juice with ginger, shallots, and garlic until it becomes a glaze. Add sambal to taste. Set aside and cool strain mixture. Whisk in grapeseed oil and miso paste. Season with salt and pepper to taste.

5 **Final Preparation and Putting it Together:** In a skillet or wok, add oil and deep fry panko-coated tuna roll until golden brown (do not over-fry). Tuna should be cooked medium-rare.

6 Cut tuna roll into four pieces. Garnish with enoki mushrooms, pea shoot sprouts and blood orange segments (optional).

Wasabi, panko, nori wrapper, enoki mushrooms, and pea shoots are all available at Asian markets and some specialty food shops.

8 ounces sushi-grade bluefin tuna

1 teaspoon wasabi paste (Japanese horseradish)

1 dried nori wrapper

1/2 cup carrots, zucchini, and yellow squash, julienned and blanched

1/2 cup tempura flour mix (for coating and frying)

Panko (Japanese bread crumbs)

1/2 cup blood orange juice

1/2 teaspoon ginger root, peeled and roughly chopped

1/2 teaspoon shallots, peeled and roughly chopped

1/2 teaspoon garlic, peeled and roughly chopped

Sambal (chile-based seasoning)

3 tablespoons grapeseed oil

2 tablespoons miso paste

Salt and pepper (to taste)

Vegetable oil (for frying)

For the Garnish:

Enoki mushrooms

Pea shoot sprouts

Blood orange segments

900 Beacon St., Boston, MA
(617)247-1500

2067 Mass Ave., Cambridge, MA
(617)492-6900

The first of two Elephant Walk restaurants opened in Union Square, Somerville in August 1991. Overwhelming success of their innovative French Cambodian Cuisine and critical acclaim led to the opening of a second Elephant Walk on Beacon Street in Boston in 1994, and a Cambodian Tapas-style restaurant in Waltham in December 1997.

Located just minutes from historic Fenway Park, the Elephant Walk on Beacon Street attracts gourmands from all walks of life, a clientele as diverse as their menu. Specialties include Rare Pan Seared Tuna Loin Over Spiced Red and Green Chili Cream Sauce.

The Somerville restaurant was recently moved to Massachusetts Avenue in Porter Square, Cambridge. The Elephant Walk owner/operators, Longteine and Kenthao de Monteiro, continually strive to provide a combination of the best Cambodian and French culinary traditions.

A light and delicious Cambodian chicken dish - serve with Jasmine Rice

Lemongrass Chicken

PrepTime: 195 minutes
Cooking Time: 10 minutes
Servings Per Recipe: 4

1 **Stock:** In a stockpot, simmer bones, onion, carrots, celery, and bay leaves in 1 1/2 gallons water for 3 hours

2 **Lemongrass Paste:** Lightly chop lemongrass, galangal, lime leaf, garlic, shallot, cilantro and turmeric. In a food processor (or blender), puree with 1/4 cup water until smooth.

3 **Chicken:** Remove cartilage from breast meat and cut into 1/2-inch strips. In a medium-hot sauté pan, sear chicken on all sides. Add sugar, salt, onion, pepper and scallion; sauté for 2 minutes. Gradually add 1/4 cup chicken stock and 3 teaspoons lemongrass paste; simmer mixture to sauce consistency.

Crushed red pepper may be added for a spicy flavor addition.

For the Chicken Stock:

5 lb bones, to simmer in 1 1/2 gallons water for 3 hours

1 cup onion, peeled and diced

1 cup carrots, peeled and chopped

1 cup celery, chopped

2 bay leaves

For the Lemongrass Paste:

2 stalks lemongrass (discard outer leaves, root, and tip)

1 tablespoon galangal, peeled and chopped

1 kaffir lime leaf (center vein removed)

2 tablespoons garlic, peeled and chopped

1 tablespoon shallot, peeled and chopped

1/4 cup cilantro leaves

1/2 teaspoon turmeric

For the Chicken:

4 (6-ounce) chicken breasts, boned and cut into 1/2-inch pieces

3 teaspoons sugar (or to taste)

1 teaspoon salt (or to taste)

Spanish onion, peeled and cut into small julienne

Red pepper, seeded deveined and cut into small julienne

Scallions, trimmed and cut into small julienne

Chopped peanuts (for garnish)

Orange roughy filets wrapped in potatoes and accompanied by Sweet & Sour Tomato Sauce

BERNARD'S

506 S. Grand Ave., Los Angeles , CA
(213)612-1580

Bernard's at the historic Regal Biltmore Hotel is located off Rendezvous Court. Bernard's award-winning Continental Cuisine features an epicurean selection of grilled seafood and meats in an elegant wood-panelled setting.

Only minutes away from the Music Center, Bernard's offers the perfect location for pre-theater dining or a romantic evening getaway for two. Bernard's has been the recipient of numerous awards including being voted among the "Top 50" restaurants in the nation by readers of Condé Nast Traveler, and voted among the "Top 20" restaurants in Los Angeles by Gourmet Magazine's reader survey.

The menu, under the guidance of Executive Chef Roger Pigozzi, features Continental Cuisine with an emphasis on fresh fish, seafood and game. In addition, Bernard's offers the "Chef's Table," a special menu prepared by Chef Pigozzi and served in the legendary Regal Biltmore kitchen for groups of as many as 40. At 25,000 square feet, the kitchen is one of the largest in Los Angeles.

Orange Roughy Wrapped in Potatoes

PrepTime: 10 minutes
Cooking Time: 20 minutes
Servings Per Recipe: 4

2 pounds orange roughy, filets

4 large potatoes, peeled and grated to fine julienne

2 cups salad oil

3 teaspoons salt (or to taste)

1 teaspoon white pepper (or to taste)

For the Sauce:

1 tablespoon sugar

1/2 cup balsamic vinegar

1 cup tomato juice

1/2 cup clam juice

Salt and pepper (to taste)

1 Season the potatoes and fish with salt and pepper, to taste. Heat oil in saucepan over medium heat, until hot. Place a layer of grated potatoes in the saucepan; add a thin piece of fish filet on top. Place another thin layer of potatoes on top of fish. Cook on one side until golden brown (approximately 5 minutes over medium heat). When first side is done, carefully turn and cook on other side. When done, transfer to warm serving dish making sure excess oil has been drained. Complete the procedure with remaining fish.

2 **Sauce:** In a saucepan, caramelize the sugar. Add vinegar and boil for 3 minutes. Add tomato juice and clam juice and return to a boil. Continue to boil for an additional 3 minutes. Adjust seasonings with salt and pepper.

This zesty grouper has a hint of saffron and is accompanied by flavorful plantains

NEW WORLD CUISINE

CHEF ALLEN'S

19088 N.E. 29th Avenue, Aventura, FL
(305)935-2900

Chef Allen's Restaurant specializes in New World cuisine. The award-winning restaurant's menu changes daily and features fresh local fish and tropical fruits and vegetables.

Their signature dish is the souffle and they offer an array of interesting and different selections, one for each night of the week.

An excellent and extensive wine list, including a wide selection of wines by the glass, perfectly complements the menu.

"Award of Excellence" - The Wine Spectator

"Best Wine by the Glass in Miami" - Food and Wine Magazine

"Ponce de Leon" - New World Cuisine

"Best Chef in the Southeastern United States" - The James Beard Foundation

Mustard Seed Crusted Grouper with Plantains

PrepTime: 25 minutes
Cooking Time: 60 minutes
Servings Per Recipe: 4

1 **Plantains:** Preheat the oven to 325°F. Coat the plantains lightly with 1 teaspoon of olive oil. In an oven-proof dish, roast the plantains for 1 hour (until soft). Remove from oven.

2 When plantains are cool enough to handle, peel and slice on the bias (1-inch thick). Sprinkle generously with brown sugar, peanuts, freshly squeezed lime juice and rum; keep warm.

3 **Sauce:** In a medium sauce pan, combine the saffron, orange juice, mustard, and Sauterne. Over medium heat, simmer sauce until reduced by half. Remove from heat source and keep warm.

4 **Grouper:** In a heavy bottomed sauce pan, warm olive oil. Season the grouper with pepper and salt, then liberally press the mustard seed onto the fish. In a skillet, pan fry the grouper, browning both sides (about 2-3 minutes per side) until cooked through.

5 **Putting it Together:** Pour the sauce in the center of each plate. Place the plantains on sauce. Place the grouper on top, and garnish with fresh cilantro.

For the Plantains:

4 medium yellow plantains

1/3 cup olive oil

1/4 cup brown sugar

1/4 cup salted roasted peanuts, chopped

Juice of 1 lime

2 tablespoons spiced rum

For the Sauce:

1/8 teaspoon saffron threads

1/2 cup fresh orange juice

1 teaspoon coarse grain mustard

2/3 cup Sauterne

For the Grouper:

4 (6-ounce) grouper filets

1 teaspoon cracked black peppercorns

1 tablespoon kosher salt

2 tablespoons black mustard seeds

3 tablespoons cilantro, chopped

This doubled process smoked filet is elegant and exotic

FIVE FEET

CONTEMPORARY ·· CHINESE ·· CUISINE

328 Glenneyre St., Laguna Beach, CA
(949)497-4955

With its sandy beaches and rocky cliffs, the seaside village of Laguna Beach has long been a favorite destination for those seeking a break from the busy world.

Laguna Beach is also well known as an artist colony, and lately, a certain Laguna Beach restaurant has been gaining recognition in its own right. The Five Feet restaurant, playing off the Laguna Beach's artist colony theme, has created an art gallery setting and exhibition kitchen. Here, celebrated Chef Michael Kang prepares contemporary Chinese cuisine.

Five Feet has been consistently rated with the top restaurants by Zagat and has received rave reviews from The New York Times, Los Angeles Times and Gourmet Magazine.

Winner, Gourmet Magazine National Cook-Off

"Gold Award" Southern California Restaurant Writers

"Award of Excellence" California Restaurant Writers

James Beard Foundation Award

Twice Cooked Prime Filet

PrepTime: 120 minutes
Cooking Time: 30 minutes
Servings Per Recipe: 4

3 pounds filet of beef tenderloin (ask butcher for châteaubriand cut)

For the Filet Marinade:

1/2 quart water
1 quart soy sauce
1 cup mushrooms, cleaned and chopped
3 strips ginger root, peeled and smashed
1 cup Chinese whiskey (or cream sherry)
2 tablespoons Szechuan peppercorns, burned
1 bunch green onion, trimmed and cut into lengthy strips
10 dry chiles (or to taste)
1 cup brown sugar (rock sugar)
1/2 cup black vinegar
1 teaspoon white pepper
1/2 cup sesame oil
10 whole star anise

For the Smoking Ingredients:

1 cup rice (uncooked)
5 whole star anise
1 tablespoon Szechuan peppercorns
2 tablespoons jasmine tea
1/2 pound brown sugar
6-8 dried chiles (or to taste)

For the Asian Mango Papaya Chow Chow:

8 oz each: mango and papaya (medium diced)
1/2 medium red onion, peeled and diced
2 green onions, trimmed and chopped
1 tablespoon cilantro, chopped
1 tablespoon fresh basil, chopped (use Thai basil if possible)
1/2 teaspoon fresh ginger, peeled and minced
1/2 teaspoon fresh mint, minced
1 red jalapeño pepper, diced
2 tablespoons honey
1 tablespoon fish sauce
1 teaspoon rice vinegar
1/2 teaspoon hot oil (or to taste)
Juice of 1 lemon and 1 lime
Salt (to taste)

1 **Marinade**: In a large container, mix together water, soy sauce, mushrooms, ginger, whiskey, peppercorns, onion, dry chile, brown sugar, vinegar, white pepper, sesame oil and star anise. Submerge filet completely in marinade; leave to marinate for 2 hours (do not exceed the 2 hour limit). Remove filet from marinade and pat dry. Place in refrigerator.

2 Remove filet from refrigerator 1 hour prior to smoking to bring beef temperature even with room temperatures (except for extremely hot days).

3 **Tea Smoking**: Prepare wok - place aluminum foil or wax paper onto bottom of wok. Place uncooked rice on top of foil or paper to weight it down.

4 In a bowl, mix together star anise, Szechuan peppercorns, jasmine tea, brown sugar and chiles. Spread evenly the mixed ingredients over foil or wax paper. Place wire rack on top of dry ingredients. Place marinated filet on wire rack; cover with plate or lid that will fit inside of wok. Place damp towel around lid to keep smoke from escaping.

5 Smoke with flame for 10 minutes. Turn off flame and let smoke for 10 more minutes. Place filet into freezer immediately to cool. One half hour prior to serving, set oven for 375° F. Roast filet for 10 minutes; let filet rest for 10 minutes before slicing and serving.

6 **Chow Chow**: In a large bowl, mix together mango, papaya, red and green onions, cilantro, basil, ginger, mint, jalapeño, honey, fish sauce, vinegar, hot oil, lemon and lime juice, and salt (to taste). Mix well; set aside in refrigerator. Spoon over filet before serving.

Additional equipment needed: wok and wire rack.

Dover sole served with crayfish, chanterelles, and sprouts in a lobster basil emulsion

429 Temple, Highland Park, IL
(847)432-0770

With its comfortable, understated elegance, Carlos' has earned a reputation as a wonderful place to celebrate special occasions like birthdays and anniversaries.

Located in a small, charming building in Highland Park, the intimate and romantic restaurant has been delighting patrons for 17 years with such Contemporary French dishes as Roulade of Dover Sole with Crayfish Chanterelles or Oven Roasted Fig-Glazed California Squab. And, there's always an excellent wine selection from Carlos' award-winning wine list to accompany any entree.

"Grand Award" - Wine Spectator

DiRoNA Award

"Four Stars" - Chicago Magazine

4 Stars - Chicago Tribune

Zagat Survey

Gourmet Magazine

North Shore Magazine

Food & Wine Magazine, One of the Top 25 Restaurants in North America

WBBM Radio 20 out of 20

Mobil Award - Four Diamonds

Roulade of Dover Sole

PrepTime: 60 minutes
Cooking Time: 10 minutes
Servings Per Recipe: 4

1 **Filling:** In a food processor fitted with the steel "s" blade, combine 3/4 cup crayfish, butter, garlic, chipotle powder, cream, Armagnac, tarragon, basil, mint, corn flake crumbs, breadcrumbs, salt and pepper; pulse to puree and combine thoroughly (do not let mixture get too soft by over-processing). When smooth, add remaining crayfish and pulse briefly to shred and combine, leave meat visible.

2 Lay flattened filets skin side up, thinly spread filling mixture evenly over each. Starting from the tail, carefully roll each filet (making roulade) and pin with 2 toothpicks evenly spaced to hold filet secure. Place on a plate, cover, and refrigerate until ready to use.

3 **Sauce:** In a 2-quart sauce pot, lightly sauté shallot and garlic in minimum amount of oil. Add stock and cream; reduce by three-fourths (until sauce lightly coats the back of a spoon). Remove from heat, add basil and season with salt and pepper to taste. Before serving, strain through a chinois (fine mesh strainer) and skim any fat that may rise to surface. Keep warm in a warm water bath until ready to use or refrigerate overnight and reheat gently.

4 **Vegetables:** In a medium-size sauté pan, heat oil to sauté and lightly brown delicata squash. Add mushrooms, Brussels sprouts and seasonings; heat thoroughly. Add butter if mixture seems dry - then add shallots and chives and continue to heat. When ready to serve, add sprouts and toss frequently over heat. When sprouts are warmed but still crisp, check seasoning and adjust if necessary. Divide evenly among 4 plates.

5 **Final Preparation and Putting it Together:** Preheat oven to 400° F and turn broiler on. Heat large non-stick oven-ready sauté pan over medium-heat; add oil. Place roulades in pan standing on end and sauté until lightly browned. Turn over and place in oven for 3 minutes.

6 Remove pan from oven and take fish out of pan and place on cutting board. With a sharp knife, cut each roulade into 2 rounds in between the toothpicks. Place rounds on a lightly buttered pan and place under broiler for about 1 minute or until lightly browned but still very moist. Remove from pan, carefully remove toothpicks, place 4 rounds on a bed of vegetable mixture and spoon sauce around.

2 fresh Dover sole, fileted and slightly pounded thin (8 filets)

For the Filling:
1 cup cooked crayfish tails, cooled
3/4 cup unsalted butter, slightly softened
1 teaspoon roasted garlic puree
1/2 teaspoon chipotle powder
1/4 cup heavy cream
1/8 cup Armagnac (French brandy)
1/2 teaspoon minced fresh tarragon
1/2 teaspoon minced fresh basil
1/2 teaspoon minced fresh mint
1/2 cup corn flake crumbs
1/4 cup plain breadcrumbs
Salt and pepper (to taste)

For the Sauce:
1 shallot, roughly chopped
2 cloves of garlic, peeled and smashed
1 tablespoon olive oil
3 cups reduced lobster stock
1 cup heavy cream
Basil leaves and stems

For the Vegetables:
1/2 cup delicata squash, diced, blanched and cooled
Olive oil
1/2 cup chanterelle mushroom, cleaned and cut into small pieces, sautéed, seasoned and cooled
1/2 cup Brussels sprouts, blanched, cooled, and sliced into rounds
2 tablespoons butter (to sauté and reheat)
1 tablespoon minced shallots
1 tablespoon minced chives
1/2 cup pea or daikon sprouts, cut into 1-inch length
1/2 cup radish sprouts
Salt and white pepper (to taste)

Additional Equipment:
Toothpicks

What sounds like a side dish is a lovely light entree or special appetizer

L'Auberge Chez François

332 Springvale Rd., Great Falls, VA (703)759-3800

Alsace-Lorraine has produced one of the world's richest and most varied cuisines. It combines traditional French cooking with surprising and delicious ingredients. François Haeringer and his son, Jacques, have captured the flavor of Alsace in the hills outside Washington, D.C., home of L'Auberge Chez François, acclaimed "Best Restaurant in Washington" for eight straight years by the readers of The Washingtonian Magazine. Roland R. Mesnier, pastry chef at The White House writes "L'Auberge Chez François has been for many years my favorite restaurant and the favorite of many Washingtonians. What a treat to have Jacques Haeringer's wonderful recipes in such a beautiful book." He referred to The Chez François Cookbook by Jacques E. Haeringer. The restaurant opened April 20, 1976 and the youngest brother, Paul, joined the staff in 1979. "Paul's arrival completed my father's dream of a family-run auberge," writes Jacques. The cuisine includes classics enjoyed by patrons for over 30 years, adaptations of regional American dishes, and current recipes.

Alsatian-Style Fresh Asparagus

PrepTime: 10 minutes
Cooking Time: 20-30 minutes
Servings Per Recipe: 4

2 quarts water

2 tablespoons salt

Bay leaves

Cloves

2 lb fresh jumbo asparagus

4 veal scallopini (cut from top round)

Salt and freshly ground black pepper

All-purpose flour

1 stick butter

1 tablespoon vegetable oil

4 slices dry cured ham

1 tablespoon red wine vinegar

2 teaspoons capers

8 tablespoons grated Gruyère cheese

2 hard-boiled eggs

4 sprigs parsley

Additional Equipment:

Kitchen mallet (optional)

1 In a saucepan, combine the water with the salt, bay leaves, and cloves and simmer for 15 minutes. Peel asparagus, cut off tough lower stems. Lay asparagus in a deep pan so that all tips are facing in the same direction. Cover asparagus with prepared seasoned water, bring to a boil and simmer 5-6 minutes. Drain at once on towels.

2 Preheat broiler. Pound veal to an even thickness (1/4-inch) with flat side of a meat cleaver (or kitchen mallet). Season meat with salt and pepper, and dredge in flour, shaking off the excess.

3 In a large sauté pan, combine 2 tablespoons of the butter and 1 tablespoon oil over high flame until butter begins to brown. Add veal and sauté quickly on both sides until lightly browned (1-2 minutes). Remove veal and keep warm. Add slices of ham and lightly sauté (about 20 seconds on each side).

4 Place a slice of veal and a slice of ham side by side on warm dinner plates. Arrange asparagus on top of meat and sprinkle with vinegar and capers. Top with grated cheese. Place prepared plates under broiler to brown the cheese.

5 Brown remaining butter. Remove plates from broiler and pour browned butter over asparagus. Garnish each plate with two quarters of hard-boiled egg and a sprig of fresh parsley. Serve immediately.

Use your favorite grated cheese in place of the Gruyère - keep in mind, some cheeses have a higher salt content than others.

Jamison lamb and lobster in a roasted pumpkin with beurre blanc sauce

Grand Floridian Resort & Spa,
Lake Buena Vista, FL (407)824-1089

Victoria & Albert's Restaurant is an award-winning restaurant featuring two world class menus.

Chef Scott Hunnel tailors each course to perfection, from the luxury ingredients through preparation and plate design, to its presentation. His creations are truly something to behold.

An expertly appointed wine list assures your choice of the perfect wine to accompany your meal.

"Chefs to Keep Your Eye On" - Esquire

"Rising Star of American Cuisine" - Wine Spectator

"Top Ten in U.S.A." - Zagat Guide

"Top Ten Tables to Dine At" - Robb Report

Roasted Lamb and Lobster with Beurre Blanc

PrepTime: 360 minutes
Cooking Time: 60 minutes
Servings Per Recipe: 6

1 **Veal Stock:** Place the bones in a roasting pan in a hot oven at 375° F and brown them well. This will take 1 to 2 hours. Remove bones from pan and place in a stock pot. Cover with water and ice and bring to a simmer. Drain and reserve the fat in the roasting pan. Deglaze the pan with red wine and add to stock pot. Toss the onions, carrots, and celery with some of the reserved fat and brown well in the oven.
2 Add the browned vegetables, the tomato product, garlic, leek and herbs to the stock pot. Continue to simmer for a total cooking time of 4 hours, skimming the surface as necessary. Add water as needed to keep bones covered.
3 Strain stock through a chinois (fine mesh strainer) lined with several layers of cheese cloth. Cool the stock in a cold water bath and refrigerate overnight. The next day, skim all the remaining fat off the top of the stock. Place the stock back into a pot and reduce by 1/2 its original volume by simmering. This will take 1 to 2 hours. Skim the stock while reducing.
4 **Beurre Blanc:** In a sauce pot, reduce white wine and shallots until 1 tablespoon is left; add cream, cook down by half the volume (approximately 10 minutes) over medium heat. Remove from heat source and slowly whisk in butter. Season with salt and pepper.
5 **Vegetables:** Preheat oven to 400° F. Place 1 teaspoon each brown sugar and butter and a pinch of allspice into each pumpkin. Roast in oven for 30 minutes.
6 In a small pot of simmering water (2 cups water), add 2 tablespoons butter and 1 pinch of salt and pepper. Cook all vegetables in simmering water for approximately 3 minutes.
7 **Lamb and Lobster:** In a large pot of water, enough to submerge the lobsters, place lobsters into boiling water. Cook for 10 minutes. Pull out, de-shell lobster and keep warm.
8 Season lamb with salt and pepper, grill to desired temperature. Slice to create 3 bone racks.
9 **Putting it Together:** Place pumpkin on plate. Stuff with desired mashed potatoes (using a pastry bag). Place lobster inside and arrange vegetables in pumpkin (as shown in photo). Place lamb and claw on plate; drizzle or pour sauce on plate. Add final touches with the fresh herbs. Repeat with remaining pumpkins.

The veal stock is generally made the day before. Additional information: 1) Browning bones, the darker you can get them, without burning - the darker the final au jus. 2) Covering the roasted bones in ice water helps release the gelatin and yields a more flavorful au jus.

For the Veal Stock:
10-12 pounds lamb bones (cut into 3-4-inch pieces - butcher will cut for you)
10-12 quarts ice cold water
1 bottle Burgundy wine
1 lb onions, peeled and chopped
1 cup carrots, peeled and chopped
1 cup celery, chopped
1 lb tomatoes (or tomato puree)
2 cloves garlic, peeled and chopped
1 leek (white part only), sliced
6-8 parsley sprigs
1/4 teaspoon thyme
1 bay leaf

For the Beurre Blanc:
1 cup white wine
2 teaspoons shallots, peeled and chopped
1 cup heavy cream
1 cup butter, cubed
1 teaspoon salt
1/4 teaspoon pepper

For the Vegetables:
6 mini pumpkins, tops removed and cavity cleaned
6 teaspoons brown sugar
1/2 lb butter (divided)
6 pinches allspice
Pinch of salt and pepper (or to taste)
1 mini green zucchini
3 baby carrots
18 English peas
18 asparagus, peeled
18 yellow wax beans
6 chives

For the Lamb and Lobster:
3 live Maine lobsters (2 1/2-lbs each)
3 lamb racks, cleaned and frenched (have butcher clean)
Salt and pepper (to taste)
6 fresh basil leaves
1 cup lamb jus
Mashed potatoes (Yukon Gold or sweet potatoes), prepared

Lamb Chops with Strada & Nicoise Olive Truffle Vinaigrette

Cafe Allegro

1815 W. 39th St., Kansas City, MO (816)561-3663

Cafe Allegro has a long-standing award list in many categories from renowned food and wine critics. This chic bistro is considered Kansas City's most fashionable dining establishment for over a decade. Known for a casual, elegant atmosphere and intimate dining, Cafe Allego offers a very imaginative contemporary menu that transcends any one cuisine. It incorporates a variety of unique preparation methods and flavors. Stephen Cole's signature style of cooking has received national acclaim. The staff at Cafe Allegro will see to it that your dining experience is also nothing less than "award winning." For the dining experience that is truly exceptional in all aspects, Cafe Allegro is the choice of the most respected restaurant critics.

"Kansas City's Favorite Restaurant, Best Food, Best Service-1991, 1993, 1995, 1997" - Zagat Restaurant Survey

DiRoNa Award-1992, 1993, 1994, 1995, 1996, 1997, 1998

Grilled Rack of Lamb with Vegetable Strada

PrepTime: 60 minutes
Cooking Time: 25 minutes
Servings Per Recipe: 12

1 **Lamb:** In a mixing bowl, combine herbs, black pepper, garlic, and olive oil. Rub marinade all over each trimmed rack and set aside for grilling. When ready to grill (time it with your strada) - place marinated racks over prepared grill and cook to desired doneness.

2 **Vegetable Strada:** Dry out rounds of bread (set out overnight or baked in a 200° F oven for 1 hour). Set aside for assembly. In a 4-quart stainless steel sauce pot, heat 2 tablespoons olive oil. Add onions and cook over medium heat until translucent. Add garlic; stir and cook until aromatic (do not brown garlic). Add pear tomatoes and cook over low heat for 1 hour. Add sugar and oregano; season with salt and pepper, to taste. In a blender or food processor, puree sauce and set aside to cool. In a heated skillet with olive oil, brown the crimini mushrooms, then toss with garlic tomato sauce, and set aside to cool. In a heated skillet with olive oil, cook the diced peppers, zucchini, and eggplant until soft (5 minutes) and set aside to cool. Make custard by combining eggs, milk, and nutmeg. Assemble strada in 12 (8-ounce) ramekins (spray ramekins with non-stick cooking spray) - in the following order: 1 tablespoon tomato sauce, bread round, criminis, Asiago, bread round, 1 tablespoon tomato sauce, zucchini, peppers, eggplant, Asiago, spinach, bread round, 1 tablespoon tomato sauce, crumble of blue cheese; fill ramekin with custard. Bake in 400° F oven for 15-20 minutes. Flip out of ramekins onto serving plate.

3 **Vinaigrette:** In a nonreactive mixing bowl, combine vinegar, shallots, oregano, and garlic; slowly whisk in oils, then Nicoise olives.

4 **Putting it Together:** Rough chop radicchio and friseé. In a bowl, toss salad greens with vinaigrette. Arrange salad around strada on plate, then lean chops of grilled lamb against strada. Garnish with rosemary sprig or oregano.

Truffle oil and truffle vinegar can be purchased at specialty food shops.

For the Lamb Marinade:
12 racks of domestic lamb (4 chops each), frenched and trimmed
1/2 cup Italian parsley, minced
1/4 cup sage, minced
1/4 cup oregano, minced
1/4 cup thyme leaves
1/2 cup garlic, peeled and minced
1/4 cup freshly cracked black pepper
1/2 cup olive oil

For the Vegetable Strada:
36 (4 x 1/4-inch) rounds of French Farm Bread
Olive oil
1 onion, peeled and chopped
1/3 cup garlic, peeled and minced
6 cups pear tomatoes, in juice
2 tablespoons sugar
2 tablespoons oregano, minced
1 lb crimini mushrooms, thinly sliced
4-6 Anaheim peppers, seeds removed and cut into small dice
2 medium zucchini, seeds removed and cut into small dice
1 medium eggplant, seeds removed, and cut into small dice
Non-stick cooking spray
8 eggs
4 cups milk
1 teaspoon nutmeg
1 cup Asiago cheese, freshly grated
1 cup spinach, sautéed with 1 teaspoon garlic and drained
1 cup Maytag blue cheese

For the Nicoise Olive Truffle Vinaigrette:
1 cup extra virgin olive oil
1/4 cup white truffle oil
1/2 cup black truffle vinegar
2 tablespoons shallots, peeled and minced
2 tablespoons oregano, minced
1 tablespoon garlic, peeled and minced
Freshly cracked black pepper and salt (to taste)
1 head radicchio
2 heads frisée (a variety of endive)

For the Garnish:
Rosemary or oregano sprigs

Additional Equipment:
12 (8-ounce) ramekins

For that very special dinner for two - this lobster and herbed risotto is simply perfect

1232 W. Paces Ferry Rd., Atlanta, GA
(404)261-3662

Award-winning Pano's & Paul's is rated one of the top restaurants in the country for service. Open since 1979, Pano's & Paul's continues to provide a familiar yet exotic dinner menu, superior food presentation, a thoroughly experienced staff and a warm, plush interior.

They are not only renowned for the way they pamper their guests with unflappable European-style care in lavishly chic settings, but for their innovative yet comforting food prepared by highly trained chefs.

Pano's & Paul's American/Continental cuisine is enticing. According to Atlanta Magazine's food critic Christiane Lauterbach, "Pano's & Paul's is an institution, an Atlanta tradition. But far from dozing in the smugness of its success, the restaurant shows great vitality."

The restaurant is the flagship of the Buckhead Life Restaurant Group, which also operates 103 West, Buckhead Diner, Chops, Pricci, Veni Vidi Vici, and Atlanta Fish Market restaurant to name a few.

"4 Stars" - Mobil

"AAA Five Diamond Award"

Roasted Maine Lobster over Lemon Herb Risotto

PrepTime: 10 minutes
Cooking Time: 25 minutes
Servings Per Recipe: 2

1 **Lobster:** In a large stockpot, blanch lobster for 4 minutes. When cool enough to handle, twist off tail and cut in half; discard the intestine. Carefully crack the claw shells without breaking them up; remove meat from shell and set aside. Preheat oven and roasting pan to 400° F.

2 **Port Wine Sauce:** In a saucepan, reduce port wine and Burgundy until syrupy in consistency. Remove from heat and slowly whisk in butter; set aside.

3 **Risotto:** In a small pot, heat stock. In a medium saucepan, cook shallots in butter until transparent. Add rice, stirring until well coated, shiny and translucent. Turn up heat; add the wine. Cook over high heat until the wine evaporates. Turn the heat down, to simmer the rice. Slowly add hot stock until all the broth is absorbed in the rice. Turn off heat. Stir in cheese; season with salt and pepper to taste. Finish with lemon zest and herbs.

4 **Putting it Together:** Rub lobster tails and claws(meat) with olive oil and place on roasting pan. Roast for 5-6 minutes in preheated oven.

5 On a platter or plate, arrange lobster on top of risotto and garnish with some of the herbs and lemon zest. Finish the dish with the port wine reduction.

For the Lobster:

1 (2-pound) Maine lobster

2 tablespoons extra virgin olive oil

For the Port Wine Sauce:

1 cup port wine

2 cups Burgundy wine

8 tablespoons butter (salted)

For the Risotto:

1 cup stock (lobster or vegetable)

1 shallot, peeled and finely chopped

1 tablespoon butter

1/4 cup arborio rice

1/8 cup dry white wine

1 tablespoon Parmigiano-Reggiano cheese (or good Parmesan)

Salt and pepper (to taste)

Zest of 1 lemon

1 tablespoon parsley, chopped

2 tablespoons thyme leaves

Chicken in a rich creamy sauce with asparagus and shiitake mushrooms - a special entree

The Manor

111 Prospect Ave., West Orange, NJ
(973)731-2360

When Harry Knowles opened The Manor in the hills of West Orange on New Year's Eve 1956, he could not have known then that his dream would culminate in an establishment of which The New York Times said, "It is as close as one can get to perfection" and, more recently, "A class act ... almost too perfect to be true."

It has been a long and rewarding labor of love for Harry, Doris, Wade and Kurt Knowles. They have taken the original three rooms of The Manor and created a New Jersey dining environment that captures the timeless essence of elegance and splendor.

Now a landmark, The Manor has consistently received many coveted awards, a true indication of its superior quality standards.

"Business Executives' Dining Award"

"Grand Award" - Wine Spectator

"Four Diamond Award" - AAA

"DiRoNA Award"

Chicken Fricassée with Risotto and Vegetables

PrepTime: 30 minutes
Cooking Time: 120 minutes
Servings Per Recipe: 4

1 **Sauce:** In a large soup pot, place carrots, onion, leek, and celery root. Top with chicken and white wine. Fill the pot with water until chickens are covered. Add bay leaves, star anise, coriander, white pepper, and juniper berries. Bring to a boil over medium-high heat. Lower heat and simmer for 45 minutes. After 20 minutes, remove chickens from stock pot, and debone the breasts. Remove breast meat; set aside, returning remaining chicken to pot. When chicken is fully cooked, remove from the pot. Carefully remove all the bones and discard. Cut all of the chicken meat into small pieces and set aside.

2 Strain the broth. In a small pot, heat 2 cups of broth over medium-high heat; bring to a simmer and reduce by half. Add heavy cream and continue to reduce for 3 minutes. Mix a little cornstarch with cold water. Whisk evenly into sauce (as needed), and set aside.

3 **Risotto:** In a casserole, sauté the finely chopped shallots in olive oil with bouquet garni (tied herbs). Add rice and stir until evenly coated with olive oil. Sauté rice only until translucent. Add white wine and stir continuously. Add broth slowly while stirring. The rice is done when it is tender but firm to the bite (al dente). Remove from heat, add cheese and butter while stirring. Season with salt and pepper, to taste.

4 **Vegetables:** Peel asparagus and cut off ends. In a large pot of boiling, salted water, blanch asparagus. Remove asparagus from boiling water and place in ice water for 1 minute (to stop the cooking process).

5 In a large sauté pan, heat 1 tablespoon of butter over medium high heat. Add mushrooms. Sauté until golden brown. Season with salt and pepper.

6 **Putting it Together:** To a Dutch oven or oven proof dish add chicken pieces, asparagus, mushrooms, and sauce. Heat sauce over medium high heat. Add orange juice, zest, and ginger. Season with salt and pepper, to taste. Whisk in remaining tablespoon of butter until melted and serve.

Many ingredients can be added to risotto to make interesting dishes - seafood, meat, vegetables or mushrooms.

For the Fricassée:
4 carrots, peeled and diced
3 large onions, peeled and diced
1 leek, peeled and diced
1 knob celery root, peeled and diced
2 whole free range chickens
2 cups dry white wine
Water (as needed)
4 bay leaves
1 star anise
1 tablespoon coriander seed
1 tablespoon whole white peppercorns
1 tablespoon juniper berries
2 cups heavy cream
Cornstarch (as needed)
Zest and juice of 1 orange
1 oz fresh ginger root, peeled, grated and squeezed through a cheesecloth (retain liquid)
Salt and pepper (to taste)

For the Risotto:
3 shallots, peeled and finely diced
3 tablespoons extra virgin olive oil
Bouquet garni: sprigs of thyme, rosemary and sage tied at stem ends or in a bundle
1/2 lb superfino rice (arborio or carnaroli)
2 cups dry white wine
1 1/4 cups chicken stock
3 oz Parmesan cheese
8 tablespoons butter
Salt and pepper (to taste)

For the Vegetables:
2 bundles asparagus (white preferably)
2 tablespoons butter (divided)
8 oz shiitake mushrooms, cleaned, stems removed and sliced evenly

Rare peppered tuna on basil oil with a balsamic vinegar reduction and saffron risotto

801 5th Ave., San Diego, CA (619)234-3467

Since 1989, Fio's Cucina Italiana, the dining mecca of downtown San Diego's exuberant Gaslamp Quarter National Historic District, has been voted the county's "Favorite Italian Restaurant" every year by diners and food critics alike. The reason is simple: Fio's doesn't rest on its laurels.

Its sophisticated dinner menu changes seasonally, so guests can savor the freshest, most delightful and finest cuisine available. Its homemade pastas, breads and desserts are heavenly. Its pre-theater and special-occasion menus and nightly dinner specials are the city's most imaginative. Fio's stylish dining rooms, award-winning wine collection, comfortable lounge with full bar, delightful patio dining and gracious service are unexcelled.

Costolette di Tonno al Ventura

PrepTime: 15 minutes
Cooking Time: 20 minutes
Servings Per Recipe: 4

For the Basil Oil:

1 1/2 cups basil leaves

1/2 cup Italian parsley

1 1/2 cups blend oil

1/2 cup olive oil

For the Seared Peppered Ahi:

4 (7-ounce) ahi (number 1 grade)

1/2 cup crushed black peppercorns

1/4 cup peanut oil

For the Balsamic Glaze:

1/2 cup balsamic vinegar

For the Risotto Saffron:

3 tablespoons olive oil

1 cup onion, peeled and minced

2 tablespoons shallots, peeled and minced

2 cups arborio or carnaroli rice

1/2 cup dry white wine

1 teaspoon saffron

6 cups hot chicken stock (Homemade or prepared)

1/2 teaspoon salt (or to taste)

2 tablespoons butter, cut into small pieces

1/2 cup freshly grated Parmigiano-Reggiano cheese

Freshly ground pepper (to taste)

1 **Basil Oil: Needs to be refrigerated for 2 days prior to use.** In a large pot, blanch the herbs in boiling, salted water. Remove and shock in cold water; drain. Rough chop blanched herbs, squeeze out excess water place in blender with enough oil to cover. Puree well, slowly adding remaining oil. Pour into container and refrigerate for 2 days. Strain through a chinois (fine mesh strainer) before use.

2 **Seared Peppered Ahi:** Press ahi steaks with peppercorns. In a very hot sauté pan with peanut oil, sear ahi steaks for 10 seconds. Turn carefully and sear for 10 seconds. Remove from pan and slice.

3 **Balsamic Glaze:** In a small saucepan over medium heat, slowly reduce balsamic vinegar until syrup consistency.

4 **Saffron Risotto:** In a heavy, nonreactive skillet, heat olive oil and sauté onion and shallots until golden. Add rice and stir, to coat with oil; add wine and stir well. To the hot stock, add 1 teaspoon saffron. Add 1/2 cup of hot stock and salt to the skillet; cook stirring constantly, until all liquid has been absorbed. Continue to add hot stock in small batches (just enough to completely moisten rice) and cook until each successive batch has been absorbed, stirring constantly until rice mixture is creamy and al dente.

5 Remove from heat, whip in butter and half of the grated cheese. Season with salt and freshly ground pepper. Top each serving with additional grated cheese to taste; serve immediately.

6 **Putting it Together:** When ready to serve, place some basil oil on plate, center the risotto and fan out tuna around the rice. Dot with the balsamic reduction in whatever pattern desired.

Marinated grilled tuna with a Szechuan peppercorn sauce

2000 Sidney St., St. Louis, MO
(314)771-5777

Sidney Street Café is an indoor courtyard café with polished hardwood floors, exposed bricks, street lamps and a wonderful old-fashioned bar. Housed in a 100-year-old building, this Benton Park neighborhood restaurant has been completely renovated in keeping with its turn-of-the-century roots.

Since 1985, Sidney Street Café has been serving new American and Continental dishes, including fresh seafood, chicken, pastas and hand-cut steaks, with an emphasis on herbs, sauces and presentation.

A perfect meal at Sidney's might start with their famed Bleu Cheese Tart, or the big Stuffed Mushrooms in a light cheese sauce, followed by Lamb Chops in an oriental glaze or perfectly cooked pasta in a seafood sauce thick with mussels, shrimp and crab meat. Delicious.

A lovely garden room filled with beautiful tiles, plants and skylights is perfect for private parties.

Seared Tuna with Szechuan Sauce

PrepTime: 60 + minutes
Cooking Time: 10 + minutes
Servings Per Recipe: 4

1 **Tuna:** In a large bowl, combine teriyaki sauce, olive oil, garlic, cracked pepper, pepper flakes, chili sauce, oyster sauce, green onions, cilantro, lime juice, and ginger. Mix thoroughly. Marinate tuna for 1 hour before cooking (up to 24 hours - refrigerated).

2 In a large sauté pan or on a flat grill over high heat, sear tuna on each side to desired doneness.

3 **Szechuan Tuna Sauce:** In a large sauce pan, combine sherry, chili sauce, wasabi paste, sesame oil, orange zest, teriyaki sauce, peppercorns, and ginger. Bring to boil until wine is reduced. Add cream and bring to boil; reduce by half.

4 **Putting it Together:** On serving plate, place pickled ginger, seared tuna filet, then top with Szechuan Tuna Sauce and garnish with slivered carrots and green onions.

For the Tuna:

4 tuna filets (3-inches thick)
1/4 cup teriyaki sauce
1/2 cup olive oil
1 tablespoon garlic, peeled and crushed
1 tablespoon cracked pepper
1 tablespoon red pepper flakes
1 tablespoon Chinese chili sauce
2 tablespoons oyster sauce
1 tablespoon green onions, finely chopped
1 tablespoon cilantro, chopped
1/4 cup lime juice
1 tablespoon fresh ginger, peeled and minced

For the Szechuan Tuna Sauce:

1/4 cup sherry
1 teaspoon Chinese chili sauce
1/2 teaspoon wasabi paste
1 teaspoon sesame oil
1 teaspoon orange zest
1/4 cup teriyaki sauce
1 teaspoon Szechuan peppercorns
1 teaspoon pickled ginger, finely chopped
1/2 cup cream

For the Garnish:

Slivered carrots
Slivered green onions
Pickled ginger

A Taste Of Minneapolis

Tuna and venison ravioli with roasted mushrooms & Cabernet chipotle demi-glace

Goodfellow's

An American Restaurant

40 So. 7th St., Minneapolis, MN (612)332-4800

Located in the heart of downtown Minneapolis, Goodfellow's serves award-winning American regional cuisine in an elegant and historic Art Deco environment. Goodfellow's wine list has also brought home its share of awards.

In addition to its wonderful cuisine, excellent wine list and lovely dining room, Goodfellow's lounge is a great place to meet after work or before the show. Private dining is available for groups from eight to 80.

"DiRoNA Award"

"Four Diamond" - AAA

"Award of Excellence" Wine Spectator

Nation's Restaurant News Hall of Fame

Seared Ahi Tuna with Venison Ravioli

PrepTime: 120 minutes
Cooking Time: 8-10 minutes
Servings Per Recipe: 6

1 **Ravioli:** Place egg and water in bowl and whisk in salt. Add semolina and flour and mix in mixer with paddle attachment, or by hand. Roll out dough using a pasta machine, as thin as possible. Egg wash pasta dough. Place venison in middle of the dough and top with onion and garlic. Fold the dough over and press the dough down with fingers. Cut ravioli into 2-inch size shapes. Push out air and reserve in semolina dust.

2 **Cabernet Sauce:** Place wine, ginger, and chipotle in a saucepan, and cook until it reduces down by one-third. Add demi-glace and reduce to consistency of coating the back of a spoon; strain and reserve sauce.

3 **Roasted Shiitake:** Coat mushroom caps with canola oil and place on baking sheet. Roast in a 400° F oven until wilted (brown, not crisp). When cooked, julienne, and reserve.

4 **When Ready to Serve:** Bring a large pot of salted water to a boil - place ravioli in pot and boil for 15 seconds (making sure dough is al dente). Remove from water and rinse.

5 **Ahi Tuna:** In a skillet, add peanut oil and heat to almost smoking. Add tuna and sear on both sides - cook to desired doneness. (Chef recommends keeping it rare if sushi grade.)

6 **Putting it Together:** On a serving plate, pour some of the Cabernet sauce, top with seared tuna and garnish with shiitake mushrooms and ravioli.

For the Ravioli:

1 egg

1 2/3 tablespoon water (more as needed)

1 teaspoon salt

1 cup semolina

1/2 cup all purpose flour

1 egg, whipped (egg wash)

For the Venison Ravioli Filling:

1 1/2 cups braised venison

1/2 sweet onion, julienned and sautéed

36 cloves of roasted garlic, peeled and sliced

For the Cabernet Sauce:

1 1/2 cups Cabernet wine

1/4 cup fresh ginger, peeled and grated

1 chipotle chile

1/2 cup veal demi-glace

For the Roasted Shiitake:

12 oz shiitake mushrooms, cleaned and stems removed

2 tablespoons canola oil

For the Ahi Tuna:

1 teaspoon peanut oil

6 (3 oz each) center cut ahi tuna

Game at its finest, rubbed with coriander and pepper— topped with The Riviera Steak Sauce

THE RIVIERA

7709 Inwood Rd., Dallas, TX
(214)351-0094

Since opening its beautiful curtained French doors in 1984, The Riviera has created the perfect romantic setting for an unforgettable dining experience.

With its refined atmosphere and sophisticated menu inspired by the flavors and ingredients of Northern Italy and Southern France, The Riviera evokes the atmosphere of the elegant country inns of Provence.

While keeping an eye on the kitchen at The Riviera, Executive Chef David Holben and Proprietor Franco Bertolasi have opened the Mediterraneo, Mediterraneo at the Quadrangle and Toscana restaurants.

"Top Table and Best Food Award" - Gourmet Magazine

Inductee into the "Nation's Restaurant News" Hall of Fame

Consistently high ratings in the Zagat Guide

"Mumm's Cuvee Napa Award" Condè Nast Traveler Magazine

Top 10 New Chefs of America - Food & Wine Magazine

Cervena Venison and Tomato-Eggplant Gratin

PrepTime: 180 + minutes
Cooking Time: 20 minutes
Servings Per Recipe: 6

1 **Steak Sauce:** In a large non-reactive sauce pan, saute the onions, shallots, anchovy, and minced garlic in olive oil. Add the chopped tomato and the tomato paste, and continue to cook for 2 minutes. Place the rest of the ingredients, except for the soy sauce, salt and pepper, in the sauce pan and reduce until a sauce consistency. Remember to skim the sauce frequently.

2 Transfer sauce to a blender or food processor, and pulse on and off 4-6 times. Season with soy sauce, salt and pepper.

3 **Corriander Rub:** Puree all of the ingredients for the Coriander Rub in a food processor until ingredients are incorporated. Add extra oil if mixture seems to dry.

4 **Venison:** Coat all sides of the venison lightly with the rub. Refrigerate the venison for 3-4 hours.

5 In a large skillet over high heat, sear the venison in a small amount of olive oil. Place venison in a 350° F oven for 5-8 minutes or until medium-rare. Let stand 5 minutes before serving.

6 **Gratin:** In a large skillet, sauté the onion in olive oil; add a pinch of salt and cook until transparent.

7 Brush both sides of the tomatoes and eggplant with olive oil, and sprinkle with the rosemary and thyme; season with salt and pepper. Grill the eggplant on both sides until tender (2-3 minutes), and 1-2 minutes for the tomatoes.

8 On a lightly oiled baking sheet, place 3 slices of eggplant slightly overlapping to form a circle. Place 2 tablespoons of cooked onions on top and spread out evenly. Arrange tomatoes, on top (using both colors). Repeat 5 times with remaining ingredients. Keep in oven at 350° F until warm.

9 **Putting it Together:** Place a stack of vegetable gratin in center of plate, slice the venison 3/8 inch thick and fan 4-5 slices on top. Drizzle with sauce.

Garnish with 12 stalks of blanched asparagus sliced on a bias 1/2-inch long, diced yellow and red bell peppers and salt and pepper to taste.

For the Steak Sauce:
3 tablespoons onion, chopped
1/2 cup shallots
1 tablespoon anchovy, chopped
2 teaspoons garlic, minced
2 tablespoons olive oil
3/4 cup tomatoes, chopped
1/4 cup tomato paste
1 teaspoon chile flakes
1/4 cup + 1 tablespoon Worcestershire Sauce
1 cup molasses
2 tablespoons corn syrup
1/2 cup brandy
1/4 cup red wine vinegar
1/4 cup balsamic vinegar
1 cup veal glaze
2 tablespoons tamarind paste
1 quart demi-glace
Soy sauce (to taste)
Salt and pepper (to taste)

For the Coriander Rub:
3/4 cup cracked black pepper
1 cup garlic cloves
1 cup brown sugar
2 tablespoons kosher salt
1/2 cup thyme, chopped
1/4 cup coriander, toasted and ground fine
3/4 cup sage, chopped
1/4 cup olive oil

For the Venison:
2 1/2 lb Cervena Denver leg or Cervena loin, trimmed evenly

For the Gratin:
2 medium onions, thinly sliced
1/4 cup olive oil
Pinch salt
18 slices red tomatoes, 3/8 inch thick
18 slices yellow tomatoes, 3/8 inch thick
18 slices eggplant, 3/8 inch thick
3 tablespoons fresh rosemary, chopped
3 tablespoons fresh thyme, chopped

Lamb served on green bean and mushroom ragout with fingerling potatoes

LON's at the hermosa

5532 N. Palo Cristi Rd., Paradise Valley, AZ
(602)955-7878

LON's at the hermosa is located at the historic Hermosa Inn, a building done in the traditional hacienda-style of architecture. LON's embraces all that is Southwest, with its decor of rustic Southwestern furnishings and artifacts.

LON's also embraces contemporary American dining featuring the award-winning American Cuisine of Executive Chef Patrick Poblete.

Chef Poblete creates specialty menu items that reflect each season's bounty. To be sure of the freshest ingredients, he uses fresh produce from a 10,000-square-foot garden located on the property.

Chef Poblete's New Zealand Rack of Lamb, is accompanied by a ragout of mushrooms, corn, red bell peppers, green beans and fingerling potatoes.

"One of the top four restaurants in Phoenix" - USA Today

"Hottest New Restaurant" - National Food & Wine Magazine

"Best Brunch" - Phoenix Magazine

New Zealand Rack of Lamb

PrepTime: 30 minutes
Cooking Time: 20-40 minutes
Servings Per Recipe: 4

12 oz fingerling potatoes

Olive Oil

Salt and pepper (to taste)

1/2 cup olive paste

11-12 oz New Zealand rack of lamb

1/2 cup green beans, trimmed and cut on bias (1-inch)

1/2 cup button mushrooms, cleaned and sliced

4 oz Portabella mushrooms, cleaned and sliced

1 corn on the cob, kernels removed

1 red bell pepper, seeded, deveined and cut to medium dice

1/4 cup pea shoot sprouts

Lamb sauce or condiment of choice

1 Preheat oven to 350° F. In a bowl, toss fingerling potatoes in olive oil, salt and pepper. Place coated potatoes in a roasting pan, bake for 20-30 minutes, or until done. Set potatoes aside; keep warm.

2 Rub olive paste on lamb and season with salt and pepper. In preheated sauté pan, sear lamb and place in a preheated 350° F oven for 20-40 minutes (or cook to desired doneness).

3 In preheated sauté pan, add olive oil and sauté green beans and button mushrooms; add Portabella mushrooms. Stir vegetables and allow to cook 2-3 minutes. Add corn and red peppers; cook vegetables an additional 4-6 minutes. Season with salt and pepper, to taste.

4 **Putting it Together:** Place a generous tablespoon of vegetables in center of serving plate; top with 4-5 pieces (3 ounces per serving) of fingerling potatoes. Slice lamb rack in half and place one half on its side and other half standing up. Place pea shoot sprouts in center between two lamb portions.

5 Place lamb sauce (of your choice) or condiment (chutney) around the base, and serve.

Prepared Lamb Sauce, Chutney and Fruit Condiments are available at specialty food shops.

Mr. B's BBQ shrimp makes a great appetizer or a terrific light entree

201 Royal St., New Orleans, LA (504)523-2078

In the heart of the French Quarter, Mr. B's Bistro is a major player in the ongoing process of redefining New Orleans cooking. Louisiana is a melting pot of cultures - French, Spanish, Italian, African American, Indian and Caribbean. The culinary result is Creole Cuisine and is always evolving towards new and better taste sensations. In that spirit, Mr. B's adapts and incorporates local and regional ingredients into innovative Creole creations.

Today, Cindy Brennan, owner and operator, is proud to offer her own special take on regional Creole cuisine, strong in its flavorful ties both to New Orleans and South Louisiana.

Mr. B's embraces the challenge to serve simple and honest bistro-style food for an all-occasion business lunch, a festive jazz brunch or dinner accompanied by live piano music. Mr. B's Bistro strives to deliver a great experience.

"Best Business Lunch" - Food & Wine Magazine 1998

"Top for Business" - Gourmet Magazine 1998

Barbecued Shrimp

PrepTime: 15 minutes
Cooking Time: 10 minutes
Servings Per Recipe: 2

1 **Creole Seasoning:** In a mixing bowl add salt, garlic, black pepper, cayenne, thyme, oregano, paprika and onion. Store in an airtight container.

2 **Shrimp:** Heat a sauté pan over high heat. Put shrimp, Worcestershire, both black peppers, Creole seasoning and garlic into pan; add 3 tablespoons water to pan. Squeeze lemon half into pan; cook until shrimp are cooked half way and liquid is reduced (about 4 minutes).

3 Add butter, swirling pan gently to incorporate. Serve when shrimp are cooked through and sauce is proper consistency (about another 4 minutes).

4 **Putting it Together:** Place cooked shrimp in a bowl and pour sauce over. Garnish with hot French bread (for dipping).

Use extra Creole Seasoning on your favorite meats, fish and poultry. Will keep in an airtight container.

For the Creole Seasoning:

1 cup salt

4 tablespoons granulated garlic

4 tablespoons ground black pepper

1 teaspoon cayenne pepper

1 teaspoon thyme

1 teaspoon oregano

4 tablespoons paprika

1 tablespoon granulated onion

For the Shrimp:

8 large shrimp (with heads on)

1/4 cup Worcestershire Sauce

1 teaspoon fine black pepper

1 teaspoon cracked black pepper

1 teaspoon Creole Seasoning (see recipe)

1/2 teaspoon fresh garlic, peeled and chopped

1/2 fresh lemon

12 tablespoons cold unsalted butter (cut into 6 equal potions)

For the Garnish:

Hot French Bread

Hearty and seafood laden - make sure you have plenty of grilled French bread

48688 Victoria Lane, Oakhurst, CA (209)683-6800

Upholding the excellence of the European Grand Manor Houses, Chateau du Sureau, with its ten enchanting guest rooms, sits on nine wooded acres surrounded by beautiful hillside gardens and offers its guests a stay in the traditions of long ago.

A short stroll across the gardens leads to Erna's Elderberry House, where award-winning California-French Cuisine awaits in understated country elegance. Chef James Overbaugh's six-course prix-fixe menus change nightly based on the freshest ingredients available. His innovative food has received high ratings from the 1998 Zagat Guide. Popular cooking classes combined with wine seminars are held thrice a year, offering a dynamic, personal culinary getaway for those who wish to combine luxurious accommodations with the rewarding joy of cooking (and eating!).

The unconditional commitment to excellence has earned Chateau du Sureau the highest honor from Mobil Travel, the Five Star Award. Both the hotel and restaurant have earned the Five Diamond Award from AAA. It is also a member of the prestigious Relais & Chateaux Group.

Bouillabaisse de La Maison

PrepTime: 30 minutes
Cooking Time: 45 minutes
Servings Per Recipe: 6

1 small onion, peeled and thinly sliced

1 bulb fennel, thinly sliced

1 medium carrot, peeled and thinly sliced

2 tablespoons olive oil

1 bulb roasted garlic, with softened cloves removed and mashed (amount will depend on strength)

1 cup dry vermouth

5-6 cups fish stock

1/2 teaspoon toasted coriander seeds, lightly crushed

1/2 teaspoon fennel seeds, lightly crushed

Pinch of orange zest

Parsley

Sprig of thyme, chopped

2 bay leaves

Pinch of saffron

2 tablespoons Pernod (licorice-flavored)

1/2 pound rock shrimp

6 fanny bay oysters, shucked

1/4 pound salmon, cut into 2/3-inch pieces

2 medium tomatoes, peeled, seeded and diced

1 large russet potato, peeled, small cubed and blanched

8 stems of basil (reserve 6 leaves for garnish) chiffonade remaining

Salt and pepper (to taste)

French bread

1 In a large heavy pot, sauté onions, fennel and carrot in olive oil, until soft. Add roasted garlic and vermouth; reduce until alcohol is cooked off.

2 Add fish broth, coriander, fennel seeds, orange zest, parsley, thyme, bay leaf, and saffron. Simmer until flavors are infused. Add Pernod and lightly seasoned fish. Cook to halfway point, add tomatoes, potato cubes, and basil. Season with salt and pepper.

3 Serve bouillabaisse in warmed bowls with grilled French bread and garnish with reserved basil leaves.

Small stuffed envelopes of pasta - serve as an appetizer or light entree

D'Amico Cucina

100 N. 6th Street, Minneapolis, MN (612)338-2401

An excellent restaurant, D'Amico Cucina is at once unpretentious and elegant, serving Italian Cuisine which embodies everything that is traditional about the discipline, and yet manages to put a decidedly contemporary spin on each dish.

An award winner, D'Amico Cucina is one of Minnesota's best restaurants.

"Award of Excellence" - Wine Spectator

"DiRoNA Award"

Agnolotti

PrepTime: 180 minutes
Cooking Time: 10 minutes
Servings Per Recipe: 4

1 **Dough:** On a flat surface or bowl, make a well with flour. Add egg yolks, water, olive oil, and salt; incorporate ingredients until a dough is formed. Knead thoroughly for 10 minutes. Cover the dough with a cloth and leave to rest for 2 hours.

2 **Stuffing:** Preheat oven to 350° F. In a roasting pan, heat butter and oil; turn heat up and quickly brown the onion, carrot, and rosemary. Add the meat(s) and fry on all sides until brown. Place the roasting pan in the oven and cook for 1 hour (as needed, add some water or broth).

3 In a large pot, blanch the spinach in salted boiling water and drain. Add drained spinach to the ingredients in the oven for the last 10 minutes of the cooking time.

4 Allow ingredients to cool and pass through a mincer or food grinder. Place minced mixture in a bowl and add Parmesan, eggs, salt, pepper and nutmeg.

5 **Final Preparation - Putting it Together:** On a lightly floured surface, roll the dough out thinly into two sheets. Spoon small amounts of stuffing onto 1 sheet of dough every 1 1/2 inches (until all stuffing is used). Cover with a second sheet of dough, pressing firmly around each mound (to seal). Separate the Agnolotti with a pastry wheel and cook in a pot of boiling salted water for 5 minutes (do in batches). Drain and serve with melted butter.

For the Pasta Dough:

1 cup all-purpose flour

5 egg yolks

3 tablespoons water

1 tablespoon virgin olive oil

Salt (to taste)

For the Stuffing:

3 1/2 oz butter

1/2 cup virgin olive oil

1/2 onion, peeled and chopped

1 carrot, peeled and chopped

Sprig of rosemary

1/3 lb lean pork, cubed

1/3 lb veal (for roasting), cubed

1 rabbit leg, boned

5 oz spinach, washed well and trimmed

5 oz Parmesan cheese, grated

3 eggs

Salt and pepper (to taste)

Nutmeg (to taste)

Marinated in Grand Marnier & a citrus peppercorn sauce - serve with sweet mashed potatoes

2601 E. Atlantic Blvd., Pompano Beach, FL
(954)782-0606

Darrel Broek and Chef Oliver Saucy make a winning duo. Since bursting onto the South Florida restaurant scene in 1984, their Cafe Maxx has been a magnet for aficionados of fine food and local and national food and wine critics.

Cafe Maxx's menu could best be described as South-Floridian-Creole-Italian-French-Southwestern-Asian-Cuban. It's food with a multitude of international flavors mixed with local fish, ripe exotic fruits, and fresh produce. In other words, it's dining to the Maxx.

"Top Restaurant in Operation" - Zagat Guide to South Florida

"Award of Excellence" - Wine Spectator

"Golden Spoon Award" - Florida Trend

"Five Star Chef" - Restaurant Hospitality

Duck Breasts with Banana Chutney

PrepTime: 45 minutes
Cooking Time: 90 minutes
Servings Per Recipe: 6

1 **Duck Breasts:** Score fat on top of the duck breasts. In a small nonreactive bowl, combine salt, light brown sugar, black pepper, citrus zest, shallots, olive oil and Grand Marnier. Marinate duck breasts in a shallow nonreactive container for up to 48 hours in the refrigerator, turning occasionally to ensure even distribution of seasonings.

2 **Banana Chutney:** In a medium, heavy-bottomed sauce pan, combine banana liqueur, sugar, vinegar, rum, lime juice, pickling spice, and vanilla bean pulp. Cook for 20-30 minutes over low heat, or until liquid is reduced to a syrup consistency.

3 Add bananas to the reduction, and cook until bananas have softened and begin to break down (approximately 5 minutes). Stir in the chives and butter; season with salt and pepper to taste.

4 **Putting it Together:** Scrape excess marinade off duck breasts. In a skillet, sear the duck breasts fat-side down. Cook slowly to let the fat melt (keep the meat rare), then transfer to a hot grill and finish cooking the duck to desired doneness.

5 Slice the duck breast and serve with Banana Chutney and a side of sweet mashed potatoes.

Banana Chutney can be made 6-12 hours in advance. If keeping for more than 4 hours, top mixture with juice of 1 lime and cover tightly with plastic wrap.

For the Duck:

6 duck breasts, fat and sinew trimmed
1 teaspoon salt
1 teaspoon light brown sugar
1 teaspoon cracked black pepper
1 teaspoon orange zest
1 teaspoon lime zest
1 teaspoon lemon zest
1 tablespoon shallots, peeled and chopped
1 tablespoon olive oil
2 tablespoons Grand Marnier (orange-flavored liqueur)

For the Banana Chutney:

3/4 cup banana liqueur
1 tablespoon brown sugar
3/4 cup rice wine vinegar
3/4 cup dark rum
Juice of 2 limes
1 teaspoon pickling spice, placed in a mesh or muslin bag
2 vanilla beans, split lengthwise and pulp scraped
12 ripe bananas, peeled and cut into 1/2-inch dice
2 tablespoons chives
1-2 tablespoons butter (optional)
Salt and black pepper (to taste)

Oven-roasted tamarind flavored porkribs serve with roasted garlic chipolte mashed potatoes

A DISTINCTIVE SOUTHWEST RESTAURANT

368 Main Street, Park City, UT
(435)649-6222

Chimayo serves authentic and imaginative Southwestern Cuisine, a cuisine with incomparable integrity. The food captures the essence of the indigenous landscape - rugged, varying and vast.

Corn tortillas and pinto beans, earthy, like the surrounding desert; fresh and dried chiles - as hot as the scorching southern sun; piñon nuts - harvested in the wild, whose smoke scents the air on a cold New Mexico evening; meat and game - searing over glowing coals of mesquite wood, whose gnarled forms are visible on virtually every vista.

Even the colors of the food are direct reflections of the landscape. The tawny yellow or slate-blue corn; purple, brown, and black beans; bright green fresh chiles, or deep burnt umber and sienna - all come from the same palette used by nature in coloring the landscape.

Barbecue Chipolte-Tamarind Spareribs

PrepTime: 10 minutes
Cooking Time: 240 minutes
Servings Per Recipe: 4

1 **Barbecue Sauce:** In a small blender or food processor, puree red onion, garlic and chipoltes. Add red onion puree to pot and cook 5 minutes. Add Worcestershire, orange juice concentrate, tamarind paste, brown sugar, catsup, water, jalapeño Tabasco, and molasses; cook for 1 hour, stirring periodically.

2 **Ribs:** Season both sides of ribs with salt and pepper. In a large skillet or grill, sear both sides of meat; allow to cool. Starting at small end, roll into a tight ball and tie with kitchen string (twine).

3 Place ribs in a deep roasting pan and coat well with barbecue sauce. Cover pan tightly with aluminum foil. Roast for 4 hours at 350° F.

For the Barbecue Sauce:

1 small red onion, peeled and rough chopped

2 cloves garlic, peeled

1 (7-ounce) can chipoltes

1/2 cup Worcestershire Sauce

3/8 cup orange juice concentrate

2 tablespoons tamarind paste

1/2 cup brown sugar

1 cup catsup

2 cups water

1/4 cup green Tabasco Sauce (jalapeño-flavored)

1 cup molasses

For the Ribs:

4 1/2 pounds baby back ribs

Salt and pepper (to taste)

Additional Equipment:

Kitchen string (twine)

Hot cheese polenta and Portobello mushrooms with roasted tomatoes and parsley sauce

Eagle Rock Reservation, West Orange, NJ
(973)731-3463

Built in 1909, the Florentine-style building in Eagle Rock Reservation was used for many years as a scenic overlook offering a spectacular view of the New York City skyline.

Frederick Law Olmsted, New York's Central Park landscape architect, commented that from this vantage point "... all the intervening country can be seen as from a balloon." Now, it's magnificent as Highlawn Pavilion, refurbished with such spectacular additions to the architecture as a set of 400-year-old authentic Venetian lanterns for the bar and wine cellar and an 18th-century Belgian tapestry for the wall of the lounge.

With its French rotisserie, wood-burning Italian brick oven and open-kitchen concept, Highlawn Pavilion's cuisine is aptly described as "American Fare with European Flair."

America's Top Tables Award - Gourmet Magazine

The Best of the Best - New Jersey Monthly

4 Stars - Newark Star Ledger

4 Diamonds - AAA

DiRoNA Award - Top one percent of restaurants in North America

Mascarpone Polenta with Grilled Portobello

PrepTime: 60 minutes
Cooking Time: 30 minutes
Servings Per Recipe: 4

1 **Mushroom Marinade:** In a nonreactive container, marinate the Portobello mushrooms in olive oil, balsamic vinegar and tarragon, rosemary, or your favorite herb; let marinate for 1 hour.

2 **Polenta:** In a medium pot, add 1/3 cup olive oil, garlic, and shallots. Cook over medium heat until garlic and shallots are golden brown. Add heavy cream, chicken stock, and Mascarpone cheese - bring to a boil. Slowly add cornmeal, stirring constantly with a wooden spoon. Lower heat and cook for approximately 7 minutes until polenta is thick and creamy.

3 Remove the Portobello mushrooms from the marinating liquid. If grilling, set over prepared grill and let cook on both sides until tender (approximately 20 minutes). If the mushrooms are being roasted, place in an oven-proof dish and bake at 400° F oven for 10 minutes (or until tender).

4 **Parsley Sauce:** In a blender or food processor, mix together parsley, shallot, garlic and lemon juice, until sauce-like consistency is achieved.

5 Roast tomatoes in an oven-proof dish for 10 minutes at 400° F.

6 **Putting it Together:** On a plate, place a mushroom cap; spoon on polenta, layer another mushroom cap; add another spoon of polenta, top with a third Portobello and finish with a dollop or ball of Mascarpone. Garnish with two tomato halves and parsley leaves. Sprinkle plate with parsley sauce.

Mushrooms and polenta can be cut with a large round biscuit cutter or cookie cutter to keep uniform in size.

12 thick medium size Portobello mushroom caps

For the Mushroom Marinade:

3/4 cup olive oil

4 1/2 tablespoons balsamic vinegar

2 tablespoons tarragon, rosemary or favorite herb, chopped

For the Polenta:

1/3 cup olive oil

5 cloves garlic, peeled and chopped

3 shallots, peeled and chopped

2 cups heavy cream

1 cup chicken stock (homemade or prepared)

1 cup Mascarpone cheese

4 cups cornmeal

For the Parsley Sauce:

1 bunch parsley

1 shallot, peeled

1 clove garlic, peeled and minced

2 tablespoons lemon juice

For the Garnish:

8 plum tomatoes, halved lengthwise

Mascarpone cheese (for top) - optional

Parsley leaves

Additional Equipment:

Wooden spoon

Grilled-glazed lamb accompanied by a pesto flavored risotto

251 S. 18th St., Philadelphia, PA (215)735-6787

Opus 251 is located in the Philadelphia Art Alliance building, a nationally certified landmark built in 1915.

The setting is refined and elegant and the menu features full-flavored American cuisine with Mediterranean and Asian influences. It's a collection of Executive Chef Alfonso Contrisciani's favorite dishes, all homemade and handcrafted.

Chef Contrisciani is a certified master chef and has won numerous international culinary awards. His philosophy is to bring out the natural flavors of food. Opus 251 is an elegant and affordable place to meet and eat and to enjoy art and culture.

"Best American Restaurant of Philadelphia" - Zagat

"Best of Philly" - Philadelphia Magazine, two consecutive years

"Three Stars" - Mobil Guide

Wood-Grilled Lamb with Balsamic Mustard Glaze

PrepTime: 45 minutes
Cooking Time: 20 minutes
Servings Per Recipe: 4

For the Creamy Pesto Risotto:
4 cups chicken stock (homemade or prepared), heated
1/2 cup yellow onion, peeled and diced
2 tablespoon butter (divided)
1 cup arborio rice
1/4 cup dry white wine
1/4 cup heavy cream
1/4 cup grated Parmesan cheese
2 tablespoons pesto (prepared)
Salt and pepper (to taste)

For the Balsamic Mustard Glaze:
1/2 teaspoon garlic, peeled and minced
1 teaspoon shallots, peeled and minced
1 tablespoon olive oil
1/2 cup balsamic vinegar
1 tablespoon honey
1 cup chicken stock (homemade or prepared)
1 tablespoon mustard seed, lightly toasted
2 teaspoons cornstarch (dissolved in 1/2 tablespoon sherry)
Salt and pepper (to taste)

For the Lamb:
4 lamb top sirloin steaks
Olive oil
Cracked black pepper
Salt
1 bunch arugula, washed well and stems removed
4 plum tomatoes, cored and poached in olive oil with fresh oregano
4 tablespoons prepared eggplant caponata (optional)

1 **Pesto Risotto:** In a medium sauce pan, lightly sauté onions in 1 tablespoon of butter until translucent; add rice and evenly coat (approximately 2-3 minutes). Add white wine and one-third of hot stock - simmer rice uncovered until liquid is completely absorbed. Add remaining stock one-third at a time.

2 When all stock is absorbed, fold in cream, Parmesan cheese, prepared pesto and remaining butter. Adjust seasonings and reserve until ready to serve.

3 **Balsamic Mustard Glaze:** In a skillet, lightly sauté garlic and shallots in oil. Add balsamic vinegar, honey, and chicken stock; reduce sauce by one-fourth. Add lightly toasted mustard seeds and reduce again by one-fourth. Add cornstarch and sherry - simmer for a few minutes. Add salt and pepper to taste. Adjust thickness of sauce with additional chicken stock.

4 **For the Lamb:** Marinate lamb in olive oil, cracked black pepper and salt.

5 On a hot open grill (with wood chips) or a hot griddle skillet, cook lamb until medium-rare. Transfer lamb to a plate.

6 **Putting it Together:** In a bowl, wilt arugula in olive oil, salt and pepper - toss in poached plum tomatoes.

7 Place a mound of risotto on a plate accompanied by tossed wilted arugula and poached tomatoes. Slice lamb sirloin against the grain and shingle on risotto, top with eggplant caponata and drizzle with mustard glaze.

Caponata, a Sicilian side-dish or relish, can be purchased prepared at specialty food stores.

Unique and flavorful - salmon with lobster-red skin mashed potatoes

Hotel Rd., Hershey, PA (717)534-8800

Inspired through the travels of Milton and Catherine Hershey, the legendary Circular Dining Room offers grand opulence and the finest of culinary talents. Come experience the dream brought to life by the Hersheys. Gaze upon the beautiful formal gardens and tranquil reflecting pools just outside the 13 original handcrafted stained and painted windows.

The Chefs are masters in the art of preparing and presenting gourmet cuisine. Come experience the Four Diamond Circular Dining Room, which features contemporary American cuisine and an extensive wine list.

"Award of Excellence-1996, 1997, 1998" - Wine Spectator

Four Diamond Award for Exceptional Cusine and Service

"Favorite Restaurant-1998" - Central Pennsylvania Magazine

Salmon with Lobster-Red Skin Mashed Potatoes

PrepTime: 10 minutes
Cooking Time: 20 minutes
Servings Per Recipe: 5

1 **Salmon:** Season salmon with salt and pepper. In a hot oven proof sauté pan, sauté the salmon filets with a little butter. Put the meat side down first. Brown for 1 minute and flip to the other side. Place the pan in the oven and bake to the desired degree of doneness.

2 **Lobster-Red Skin Mashed Potatoes:** In a pot, steam the potatoes (not the red potatoes); then rice (see glossary).

3 Place the potatoes in a bowl; add the olive oil, cream, sour cream and cooked pancetta (bacon).

4 Steam the Red Bliss potatoes, add to the mashed potatoes. Add parsley, black pepper, tarragon, salt, and lobster meat; adjust seasonings and serve with the salmon.

For the Salmon:

5 (6-ounce) salmon filets

Salt and pepper (to taste)

Butter

For the Lobster-Red Skin Mashed Potatoes:

4 potatoes, peeled and steamed

1 tablespoon olive oil

1/2 cup heavy cream

2 tablespoons sour cream

3/4 cup pancetta, cut into small dice and cooked

5 Red Bliss potatoes, cut into small dice

1 tablespoon parsley, minced

1/2 tablespoon cracked black pepper (or to taste)

1/2 tablespoon tarragon, minced

Salt (to taste)

1 pound lobster meat, cooked and diced

Accompanied by foie gras ravioli, braised cabbage, and a luscious beet, beef sauce

4421 Woodward, DETROIT, MI (313)832-5700

The Whitney Mansion is an impressive former home on Woodward Avenue near downtown Detroit. The structure, completed in 1894, was designed for lumber baron David Whitney, Jr.

Created in the Romanesque style, the structure is built of South Dakota Jasper, a rare variety of pink granite which gives the outside of the house a striking rose hue.

The house became a restaurant on December 12, 1986. The Whitney currently is serving modern American Cuisine under the direction of Paul Grosz. Along with a formal serving staff, the restaurant is complemented with a Wine Spectator "Award of Excellence" wine cellar and is annually awarded the distinguished DiRoNA Award for restaurant excellence nationally.

The Whitney truly is "An American Restaurant In An American Palace."

Mushroom Dusted Sturgeon

PrepTime: 60 minutes
Cooking Time: 10 minutes
Servings Per Recipe: 4

For the Ravioli:

8 oz foie gras

3 oz cognac

Salt and ground white pepper (to taste)

8 sheets won ton wrappers

1 egg white

For the Beet Beef Sauce:

2 large beets, peeled and diced

1 cup port wine

2 cups Cabernet wine

2 sprigs fresh thyme

1 quart demi-glace (reduced veal or beef stock)

For the Sturgeon:

5 oz dried exotic mushrooms

20 oz sturgeon filet, cut into 4 equal pieces

Salt and pepper (to taste)

2 oz olive oil

For the Cabbage:

1 head savoy cabbage

10 oz bacon, cooked until crispy

1 cup veal stock (homemade or prepared)

2 oz unsalted butter

1 tablespoon fresh thyme, chopped

1 **Ravioli:** Cut foie gras into 8 (1-ounce) square pieces. Marinate with cognac, salt, and pepper for 20 minutes at room temperature. Lay out 1 won ton wrapper and brush with egg white. Place 2 pieces of liver on wrapper and cover with another. Press dough firmly with hands, cupping the liver. Cut into squares or use a round cutter (#65). Poach in boiling water (with a drop of olive oil and salt) for 30 minutes. Serve 2 with the sturgeon.

2 **Beet Beef Sauce:** In a sauce pan, reduce wines with beets until syrup consistency. Add thyme sprigs and demi-glace; slow simmer for 30 minutes. Remove thyme sprigs. Puree all ingredients in a food processor. Serve around sturgeon and cabbage.

3 **Sturgeon:** Preheat oven to 400° F. Puree dry mushrooms in a food processor (fitted with the steel "s" blade). Transfer to a blender and blend until mushrooms are 'dust'. Cover both sides of each sturgeon filet with mushroom dust. Season with salt and pepper.

4 In a skillet (with an oven-proof handle), heat olive oil over medium-high heat. Brown sturgeon on both sides and place in a hot oven for 7 minutes (or until done).

5 **Cabbage:** In another skillet, braise cabbage and bacon in veal stock and butter with fresh thyme, salt, and pepper.

6 **Putting it Together:** Slice cooked sturgeon; place on top of cabbage. Garnish with thyme sprigs and beet, beef sauce.

Flavorful and elegant - this entree is accompanied by rutabaga, lettuce & plum compote

404 North Country Rd., St. James, NY
(516)584-5999

Chef/Owner Guy Reuge obtains the perfect balance with his adventurous yet classical French Cuisine at Mirabelle, his restaurant located in an old farmhouse in St. James on Long Island.

Open since 1983, Mirabelle was practically an instant success, earning praise and adulation from Zagat and The New York Times.

Rated the second most popular restaurant on Long Island, Mirabelle is a wonderfully elegant, sophisticated and romantic place to enjoy excellent cuisine and impressive service.

Voted "Master Chef" by peers

Inductee "Maitres Cuisiniers de France"

Pheasant with Ragout of Vegetables & Compote

PrepTime: 10-12 minutes
Cooking Time: 60 minutes
Servings Per Recipe: 2

1 **Compote:** In a skillet, add plums, sugar, and cinnamon. Cook over medium heat until liquid in skillet reduces down three-quarters. Add blackberries and harrissa; cook for 5-8 minutes. Remove from heat source - keep the compote hot and add Tabasco if desired.

2 **Pheasant:** Salt and pepper inside of pheasant. Stuff pheasant with carrot, onion, and bouquet garni; salt and pepper outside. Secure the bird with kitchen twine.

3 In a roasting pan, sear the pheasant; place roaster in 425° F or until cooked and juicy (the skin should appear golden and crackling). Flambé the roasted bird with cognac. Remove bird from pan and add veal stock to roaster. Cook sauce for 2-3 minutes, strain, and reserve.

4 **Vegetables:** In a preheated skillet, add butter and rutabaga; cook over medium heat until tender. Add honey and caramelize well. Add lettuce ribs and cook for another 3 minutes. Adjust seasonings to taste.

5 **Putting it Together:** Place ragout in center of each plate. Arrange carved pheasant over ragout (1 breast and 1 leg per plate). Place 3 dollops of compote around the plate, drizzle sauce around bird and garnish with fresh herbs.

Harrissa can be purchased at specialty food shops and ethnic markets.

For the Compote:
1 pint Italian plums, pitted
1/4 cup sugar
1 cinnamon stick
1/2 cup blackberries
1 teaspoon harissa
Tabasco Sauce (a few drops or to taste)

For the Pheasant:
1 pheasant hen (2 1/2 - 3 pounds)
Salt and pepper (to taste)
1/2 carrot, peeled
1/2 onion, peeled
1 bouquet garni (parsley, celery, thyme, leeks and carrots chopped and tied in a muslin bag)
1 tablespoon cognac
1/2 cup veal stock

For the Vegetables:
1 cup rutabaga, peeled and diced
1 tablespoon butter
1 teaspoon honey
1 cup romaine lettuce (ribs cut into batonnets - match-stick shapes 1/4 x 1/4 x 2-2 1/2 inches)
Salt and pepper (to taste)

Additional Equipment:
Kitchen twine

Measurements & Equivalents

Teaspoon	Tablespoon	Cup	Fluid ounce
1	1/3	~	~
3	1	~	1/2
6	2	1/8	1
12	4	1/4	2
~	8	1/2	4
~	12	3/4	6
~	16	1	8

Note: These equivalents are approximations only.

Pinch or dash
Less than 1/8 teaspoon

2 Cups
1 pint or 16 fl oz

4 Quarts
1 gallon or 128 fl oz

4 Pecks
1 bushel

1 Stick of butter
8 tablespoons or 1/2 cup

1 Lemon
(depending on the size)
2-3 tablespoons juice or
1 tablespoon grated peel

4 Cups
1 quart or 32 fl oz

2 Gallons
8 quarts or 1 peck

1 Jigger
3 tablespoons
or 1 1/2 fl oz

4 Sticks of butter
1 lb or 2 cups

1 Slice of bread
1/2 cup bread crumbs

Fahrenheit Setting	Celsius Setting*	Gas Setting
300°F	150°C	Gas Mark 2
325°F	160°C	Gas Mark 3
350°F	180°C	Gas Mark 4
375°F	190°C	Gas Mark 5
400°F	200°C	Gas Mark 6
425°F	220°C	Gas Mark 7
450°F	230°C	Gas Mark 8
BROIL		GRILL

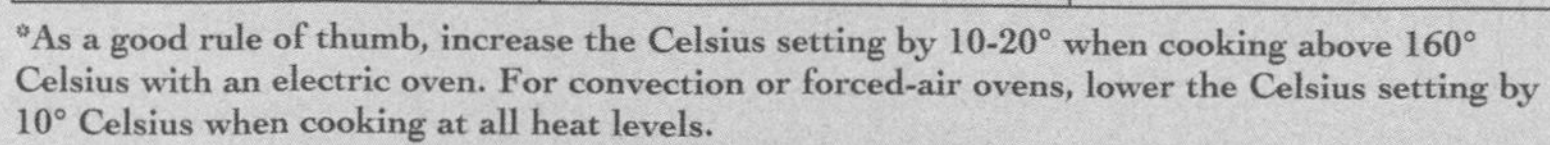
*As a good rule of thumb, increase the Celsius setting by 10-20° when cooking above 160° Celsius with an electric oven. For convection or forced-air ovens, lower the Celsius setting by 10° Celsius when cooking at all heat levels.

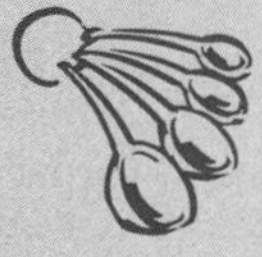

Substitutions

To truly enjoy the flavors of the recipes, it is always best to have the specified ingredients; however, when caught in a pinch, here are some suggestions...

Sorrel or "Greens"
Use spinach (equal parts)

Fennel
Use celery (equal parts)

1 Cup Sugar
Use 7/8 cup honey

Sea Salt (or any iodized salt product)
Use kosher salt (equal parts)

1 Clove Garlic
Use 1/8 teaspoon garlic powder or 1/8 teaspoon minced dried garlic or 1/2 teaspoon jarred garlic

1 Small Onion
Use 1 teaspoon onion powder or 1 tablespoon minced dried onion, rehydrated

1 Cup Tomato Sauce
Use 3 oz tomato paste plus 1/2 cup water

Sake or Rice Wine
Use dry sherry or dry vermouth (equal parts)

Fish Stock
Use equal parts clam juice and water

1 Tablespoon Fish Sauce
Use 2 teaspoons soy sauce with 2 mashed anchovies

Pancetta
Use cooked lean bacon (equal parts)

Pine Nuts
Use walnuts or almonds (equal parts)

Prosciutto
Use country ham (equal parts)

Fresh Chives
Use green onions, including the tops (equal parts)

Cocktail Sauce
Use ketchup with prepared horseradish and lemon juice (to taste)

For the Health Conscious

Use...	*In Place of...*
Anchovies	salt for salad dressings
Carrots	sugar for sauces (equal parts)
Chicken Stock	oil or fat in cooking (equal parts)
1 Cup Plain Yogurt	1 cup sour cream
7/8 Cup Vegetable Oil	1/2 lb (2 sticks) butter
Lemon Juice	salt for seasoning soups and stocks

Wine Suggestions

Red Wine

Produced from black grapes; contact between the skins and the juice during the fermentation process develops the range of color from pink to deep red.

Rosé Wine

Produced from black grapes; grape skins are left in contact with the fermenting juice just long enough to achieve the desired color. Rosé can range in hue from barely peach to an intense pink.

White Wine

Produced from white grapes (and sometimes from red grapes) having little, or no, contact between the skins and the fermenting juice—keeping it pale in color.

Sparkling Wine

(effervescent)

A wine bottled with carbon dioxide; produced by either méthode champenoise or Charmat process.

Standard Pairings

Match the wine to the strongest flavor on your plate

Rich Full Bodied Reds	*Wild Game*	Côte-Rôtie, Syrah, Zinfandel
Full Bodied to Medium Bodied Reds	*Beef, Lamb, Duck, Pasta with Red Sauce*	Red Burgundy/Pinot Noir, Cabernet Sauvignon, Merlot, Chianti Classico
Medium Bodied to Light Bodied Reds	*Pork Products and Ground Meats*	Young Bordeaux, Valpolicella, Beaujolais Cru
Light Bodied Reds	*Veal and Chicken*	Alsatian/German Pinot Noir, Beaujolais, Dry Rosé
Full Bodied/Oak-Aged Whites	*Salmon, Lobster, and Crab*	White Burgundy, Pouilly-Fumé, White Rhône, Pinot Grigio, California Chardonnay
Medium Bodied Whites	*Fish*	Chablis, Pinot Blanc, Chenin Blanc, Soave
Medium to Light Bodied Whites	*Shrimp and Scallops (small crustaceans)*	Sauvignon Blanc, Dry Riesling, Gewürztraminer
Light Crisp Wines	*Oysters and Mussels*	German Riesling, Viognier
Dessert Wines		Muscat, Late-harvest Riesling, Sauternes

Split . . . . 6.3 U.S. ounces - 187 ml
Half bottle . . . . 12.7 U.S. ounces - 375 ml
Standard bottle . . . . 25.4 U.S. ounces - 750 ml
Liter . . . . 33.8 ounces - 1 liter
Magnum . . . . 50.7 U.S. ounces - 1 1/2 liters
Standard Glass Portion . . 5 U.S. Ounces - 140 grams

Herbs, Spices and Aromatics

Basil — Ranging in both color and pungency, basil is easy to use with recipes calling for tomatoes, eggs, poultry, lamb, veal, fish, pasta, beans, grains, mushrooms, nuts, zucchini, and cheese. Delicious in salads, rice dishes, stuffing and crepes, this leaf intensifies during the cooking process.

Cilantro — Often called Chinese or Mexican parsley, cilantro is frequently used in ethnic foods. Its distinctive flavor marries well with beans, grains, rice, vegetables (salsas and salads), meats, fish, shellfish and poultry.

Coriander — With its mild slightly orange spicy-sweet flavor, this spherical seed is commonly used whole as a pickling spice or ground in recipes containing meat, rice and vegetables. The flavorful leaves are named cilantro.

Curry Powder — Traditionally used in Indian and Caribbean cuisine, its spicy flavor marries well with beans, grains, rice, vegetables, meats, fish, shellfish, and poultry. Try in chicken and vegetable-based soups.

Elephant Garlic — Members of the onion family, these cloves are milder than regular garlic, and offer a nice addition to recipes that require subtle flavor.

Ginger — Pungent and aromatic, this brown-skinned root is terrific in marinades, salad dressings, stir-fry and sushi. Great added to teas, or candied and eaten as a sweet, and marries well with cinnamon, cloves, nutmeg, garlic and chives.

Marjoram — A member of the mint family and closely resembling mild oregano, marjoram compliments the flavors of meat (all types), roasted poultry, tomatoes, green vegetables, mushrooms and pasta.

Nutmeg — This strong, flavorful seed that comes from the nutmeg tree (a type of evergreen) is generally associated with sweets; however, adds a new dimension to cream sauces and soups.

When using fresh herbs is not possible, dried herbs may be used in their place.

***~A rough estimate~
For every tablespoon of Fresh, use one teaspoon of Dried.***

Remember that less is more, so taste before adding more.

Oregano — Closely associated with wild marjoram, the distinctive and peppery flavor of oregano is commonly teamed up with thyme in a variety of recipes. Often found in Italian, Greek and Mexican cuisine, this herb often finds its way into recipes that call for tomatoes, meat sauces, beef, pork, veal and lamb.

Rosemary — The gray-green needle-shaped leaves from this branchy herb infuse the strong flavors of lemon and pine into grilled meats and fish, as well as roasted poultry.

Sage — A fragrant sub-shrub, this musty-flavored herb is often added to stuffing and savory dishes containing sausage, duck, pheasant, strong cheese and beans.

Shallots — A member of the onion family, their delicate flavor is perfect for sauces, salad dressings and marinades.

Tarragon — Common to France and Russia, its faintly anise-like flavor pairs well with vinegar for vinaigrette dressings, mayonnaise, eggs, fish and most vegetables.

Thyme — Having many species and flavors, the sprigs are often used in flavoring vinegar, meats, soups and chowders.

Turmeric — Often used in Asian and Indian cuisine, this yellow-orange slightly bitter member of the ginger family is used to give color to prepared sauces and mustard.

Glossary

Al Dente — Italian word for "to the tooth". Term used to describe pasta (also vegetables and rice) cooked to firm.

Arborio rice — Italian, short-grained rice, used in risotto. This mild white rice has a creamy consistency.

***Blanching** (blanch)* — The process of immersing food for a brief time in boiling water, then plunging into cold water to stop the cooking process. Generally, blanching is used to help remove the peel of fruits and vegetables, to remove raw flavors or to quick-cook something prior to freezing.

***Braising** (braise)* — The process of cooking meat (and sometimes vegetables) in hot fat, then placing in a covered pot with a small amount of liquid, and cooking over low heat. This process is generally used for tougher cuts of meat.

Butterfly — The technique of cutting boneless meat in a horizontal direction, without going all the way through, opening it like butterfly wings. This process is usually done by the butcher, but can easily be done by home cooks for stuffing roasts, chicken breasts, fish, or enlarging the surface of shrimp.

Caper — Unopened flower buds of a low-growing shrub Capparis spinosa, indigenous to Mediterranean areas. The green buds are pickled and used as flavorings or condiments.

***Caramelize** (caramelization)* — The natural process of cooking foods that contain natural sugar (i.e., onions) to a melting point, until they turn golden brown.

***Chinois** (China Cap)* — A kitchen tool — a fine mesh cone-shaped sieve with a handle or legs, often accompanied by a cone-shaped wooden plunger. It is perfect for fine purées (sauces and coulis) and straining stocks.

Chutney — A condiment or side dish made from fruits and vegetables and cooked with sugar, spices and vinegar — generally accompanying meat, fish or poultry. Chutney is often used with curries and ranges in texture, as well as hotness of flavor.

Clarified butter — The process of making butter clear by heating, separating and removing the milk solids (also referred to as drawn butter).

Coulis — A sauce made from a fine purée of fruits or vegetables. While used as a sauce, it makes a striking garnish.

Couscous — Native to North Africa, this grain-like pasta has become a trendy staple to fill in for potatoes or rice.

Deglaze — The process of first adding liquid to a pan that has been roasting or cooking for a period of time, and then stirring to dissolve all of the solids to liquid form. It is often used for sauces and as a base for stocks.

Demi-glace — Result of reducing brown sauce/brown stock by half — can be purchased at specialty food stores.

Glossary

***Dredge** (dredging)* — The process of coating a food with flour, finely ground crumbs or flakes (bread, cracker, cornmeal, corn flakes, etc.).

Food mill — A kitchen tool; a hand cranked sieve-like system with interchangeable disks, for the purpose of filtering and puréeing fruits and vegetables.

Garnish — To embellish or decorate a plate, platter or food with something edible. Also, a secondary food that adds flavor, texture and color to the focal ingredients.

Julienne — The process of cutting food into match stick shapes of equal size. This can be achieved by hand or with the use of a kitchen mandoline or slicer. Often used in salad, stir-fry and as a garnish.

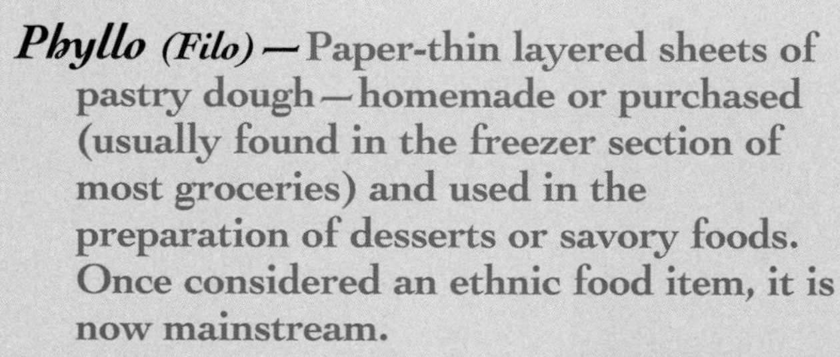

***Phyllo** (Filo)* — Paper-thin layered sheets of pastry dough — homemade or purchased (usually found in the freezer section of most groceries) and used in the preparation of desserts or savory foods. Once considered an ethnic food item, it is now mainstream.

Poaching — The process of cooking food slowly in heated liquid (i.e., wine, milk, water) below the boiling point — perfect for chicken, eggs, and fish.

***Reduce** (reduction)* — The process of quickly boiling down a liquid to enhance its flavor and transform its consistency without the use of a thickening agent.

***Ricer** (to rice)* — A kitchen tool; a handled tool that resembles a large garlic press, with the purpose of forcing cooked fruits and root vegetables into rice-size bits, free of lumps.

Roux — Equal amounts of flour and butter (or any other fat) heated together until the flour is cooked; used for thickening sauces and soups.

Score — The process of making shallow cuts in fish or meat, usually in a diamond pattern or parallel slashes, for decoration or tenderization.

Sear — The process of quick cooking food over high heat to brown — usually the first step of a multi-step cooking process. Searing does not seal in the juices; browning it does add to the overall flavor.

Whisk — A kitchen tool; handled wire loops forming a balloon-like shape, with the purpose of adding air into foods (generally eggs or egg mixtures and sauces).

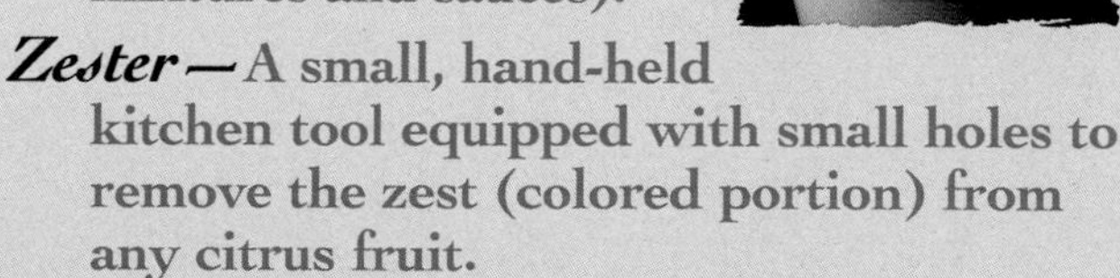

Zester — A small, hand-held kitchen tool equipped with small holes to remove the zest (colored portion) from any citrus fruit.

Coach the Cook

Apple cider can be used as a base in sauces for fowl—especially wild game birds. It is great for poaching all types of poultry or dried fruits and is delicious as a liquid in reductions. Freeze fresh cider for year 'round enjoyment; do not fill gallons to the very top.

Asparagus—To maintain freshness, keep it clean, covered and cold. Wrap stem ends in moist paper towels or stand upright in a few inches of water. Asparagus should be cooked and eaten as soon as possible as it will only keep for a few days in the refrigerator.

Cauliflower should not be cooked in aluminum or cast iron—these metals will change the color of the cauliflower. To keep it perfectly white, add lemon or lemon juice to the water.

Chiles can cause distress to the face and eyes if contact is made. The heat of the capsicum remains on hands, fingers and fingernails for long periods of time. Wear rubber or surgical gloves when seeding and deveining chiles.

Cleaning vegetables—Use a clean plastic pot scrubber or a vegetable brush.

Condiments can be easily enhanced. Transform traditional ketchup and mustard by adding herbs, spices and extracts.

Cranberries cooked in cranberry juice create a more intense flavor. When cooking them for cranberry sauce, add sugar after the berries have popped to eliminate any toughness of the skins.

Dental floss *(unflavored)* makes an excellent tress for poultry, or for cutting cheesecake clean.

Edible flowers add eye appeal and sometimes a spicy flavor to foods. Not all garden flowers are edible, so carefully check to make sure they are not poisonous and that they are bug and pesticide free. Organically grown flowers are the safest bet since flowers purchased from a florist or a specialty store are usually sprayed with toxins. Use blossoms and petals of flowers, not leaves and stems (Nasturtium leaves are an exception). Use only the petals of large flowers or small flowers whole. Edible Flowers: Anise Hyssop flowers, Arugula flowers, Basil (sweet) flowers, Borage, Calendula, Carnation, Chamomile, Chervil flowers, Chive flowers, Dandelion, Day Lily, Dill flowers, Lavender, Marigolds, Mustards, Mint flowers, Nasturtiums, Pansies (only in small amounts), Rose petals, Rosemary flowers, Sage flowers, Snapdragons, Squash blossoms, Thyme flowers and Violets.

Grease can be removed from soups and sauces by cooling down, refrigerating, then lightly placing a paper towel on top to collect the grease. It may also be removed by spooning off.

Infuse *(flavor)* olive or vegetable oil with herbs, garlic or spices. Then, for a flavor boost, sauté vegetables, fish or poultry in the flavored oil.

Juicing a lemon or lime—Prior to squeezing, press fruit firmly and roll it on a hard surface. To squeeze drop by drop, prick a small hole in the skin.

Marinate meat, fish and poultry in nonreactive containers (glass, porcelain or enamel) in the refrigerator. For food safety, do not marinate on the kitchen counter.

Meat can be sliced thin to paper-thin by partially freezing the meat prior to slicing.

Nuts can be deadly to someone who is allergic to them. Make sure whenever serving, or giving nuts as a gift, the recipient has no related allergies. If serving nuts, make sure they are fresh—they should not rattle in their shells.

Pesto can be frozen for later use. To use for pasta sauce, freeze in 1 to 1 1/2 cup containers. For flavoring in soups, stews and sauces, freeze in ice cube trays.

Plastic wrap will cling better if the rim of the container is moist.

Prepare all raw meat on a clean kitchen surface. Make sure the cutting board is cleaned with bleach water (one teaspoon of bleach to a quart of very hot water). After meat preparation, re-clean cutting board with bleach water to avoid cross-contamination.

Thaw frozen foods in the refrigerator, not at room temperature. Never leave raw food exposed at room temperature for more than one hour. To eliminate bacteria concerns, do not refreeze thawed foods.

Thicken soups and stews with quick-cooking oats—or grated, instant, or leftover mashed potatoes.

"When in Doubt—Throw it Out"—If there is any question to freshness of food (refrigerated or frozen), or foods with strange odors or appearances, discard them. Never risk food-borne illness.

Wild mushrooms should always be cooked before eating; never eat them raw. To reconstitute dried mushrooms, soak in warm water for 20-30 minutes, or overnight in cold water. Use the strained mushroom water in stocks or recipes. All mushrooms, wild or cultivated, pair well with nutmeg, butter, cream and a variety of herbs.

RESTAURANT Secrets™

RESTAURANT Secrets™ RESTAURANT Secrets™ RESTAURANT Secrets™
RESTAURANT Secrets™ RESTAURANT Secrets™ RESTAURANT Secrets™ RESTAURANT Secrets™
RESTAURANT Secrets™ RESTAURANT Secrets™ RESTAURANT Secrets™ RESTAURANT Secrets™
RESTAURANT Secrets™ RESTAURANT Secrets™ RESTAURANT Secrets™ RESTAURANT Secrets™
RESTAURANT Secrets™ RESTAURANT Secrets™ RESTAURANT Secrets™ RESTAURANT Secrets™
RESTAURANT Secrets™ RESTAURANT Secrets™ RESTAURANT Secrets™ RESTAURANT Secrets™
RESTAURANT Secrets™ RESTAURANT Secrets™ RESTAURANT Secrets™ RESTAURANT Secrets™
RESTAURANT Secrets™ RESTAURANT Secrets™ RESTAURANT Secrets™ RESTAURANT Secrets™